Garth Boomer, English Teaching and Curriculum Leadership

This book provides a broad introduction to the critical work of leading Australian educator Garth Boomer, widely recognised as a significant figure in English teaching. This insightful text provides an accessible introduction to his work, with particular reference to English curriculum and pedagogy, and provides a fascinating account of his journey as a scholar-practitioner, from classroom teaching to the highest levels of the educational bureaucracy.

Bill Green explores Boomer's huge influence on literacy education, teacher development, curriculum inquiry, and educational policy, and critically asks why Boomer's insights and arguments about English teaching from the last century have such importance for the field now. This text also focuses on the nature and significance of his curriculum thinking, specifically his arguments and provocations regarding English teaching, the English classroom, and the contexts that infuse and shape them. It constitutes a rich resource for rethinking English teaching in the present day and provides an important contribution to the historical imagination.

With all due consideration of the larger context of social life and educational thought, this text will help any student of English in education and language arts obtain a deeper understanding of Boomer's vital contribution to the field of education.

Bill Green is Emeritus Professor of Education at Charles Sturt University, Australia.

Key Thinkers in English in Education and the Language Arts

Series Editor: Andy Goodwyn

This truly global and all-encompassing series provides definitive knowledge about key thinkers in English language and literature teaching and research from around the world. Each volume is a key text to understanding the wider context to each thinker to the field, illustrating their continued relevance to contemporary approaches in English teaching and especially as it's applied to the classroom. Exploring key ideas and condensing complex theories in an easily digestible format, this series will be engaging, accessible and appealing to readers with a range of levels of interest in the field of English in Education and the Language Arts (EELA).

Titles in this series include:

L. S. Vygotsky and English in Education and the Language Arts
Peter Smagorinsky

Garth Boomer, English Teaching and Curriculum Leadership
Bill Green

For more information about this series, please visit: https://www.routledge.com/Key-Thinkers-in-English-in-Education-and-the-Language-Arts/book-series/KTEELA

Garth Boomer, English Teaching and Curriculum Leadership

Bill Green

LONDON AND NEW YORK

Designed cover image: © Getty Images

First published 2025
by Routledge
4 Park Square, Milton Park, Abingdon, Oxon OX14 4RN

and by Routledge
605 Third Avenue, New York, NY 10158

Routledge is an imprint of the Taylor & Francis Group, an informa business

© 2025 Bill Green

The right of Bill Green to be identified as author of this work has been asserted in accordance with sections 77 and 78 of the Copyright, Designs and Patents Act 1988.

All rights reserved. No part of this book may be reprinted or reproduced or utilised in any form or by any electronic, mechanical, or other means, now known or hereafter invented, including photocopying and recording, or in any information storage or retrieval system, without permission in writing from the publishers.

Trademark notice: Product or corporate names may be trademarks or registered trademarks, and are used only for identification and explanation without intent to infringe.

British Library Cataloguing-in-Publication Data
A catalogue record for this book is available from the British Library

ISBN: 978-1-032-44995-1 (hbk)
ISBN: 978-1-032-44992-0 (pbk)
ISBN: 978-1-003-37488-6 (ebk)

DOI: 10.4324/9781003374886

Typeset in Galliard
by Taylor & Francis Books

Contents

Series Editor Foreword vi
Preface viii
Acknowledgements xiii

1 Introduction and Overview 1
2 Negotiating the (English) Curriculum 15
3 'Teacher Power' – On Teachers and Teaching 37
4 Teaching English? Construing and (De)constructing the Territory 61
5 Conclusion: Neoliberal Conditions and Larrikin Lessons 78

Appendix: Ten Strategies for Good Teaching 94
References 97
Index 109

Series Editor Foreword

It is with great pleasure that I introduce the second volume in this series, 'Key Thinkers in English in Education and the Language Arts', an international series that aspires to provide truly comprehensive insights into the significance of a major author's body of work and their lasting importance to this particular field of education, but also to the development of the whole field and beyond. The series will initially focus on key figures who were of great importance to education generally and who have had strong influences on English in education, and on other leading authorities who acted directly in the field itself.

With the figure of Garth Boomer, we encounter a unique individual who unquestionably has a lasting place in the field of English in education and who followed an unusual, singular, and charismatic path. The author of this volume, Bill Green, is also uniquely placed to provide an overview and critical account of someone who he knew well, making this reflective narrative both personal in the most positive sense and holistic of what was a relatively short career, cut off at 52. Garth Boomer achieved a remarkable body of work and national and international influence in only 30 years.

Perhaps we can consider his work as a series of concentric circles? In the centre, at the core, was English and English teaching and this remained a key reference-point throughout his wide-ranging career. He was an English teacher and then a leading figure at a time when the subject of English was at its most expansive and emancipatory, in many ways it was a vision for the whole of education and profoundly concerned with the nature of schooling *per se*. The argument of visionaries like Boomer was that schooling needed to shift entirely away from the 'factory' model and the teacher as source of all knowledge to a completely different paradigm of collaboration and democratic induction; schooling was the environment in which to become an emancipated, critical, and positive citizen, and English was the key subject to drive these changes. However, this shift was not about diminishing the value of the teacher; Boomer was a constant champion of teachers and teaching – they were always at the heart of his work. What he wanted them to be was empowered to share power with students, to be autonomous so that their students would have agency, to collaborate with young people in the mutual pursuit of a fairer society.

The next circle for Boomer was the broader field of education and also the structures that controlled and managed it. Unusually, he did not move from the English classroom to teacher education or university research but into the arena of educational administration; he became what might be called a bureaucrat. But as Bill Green captures so well in this volume, that often somewhat derogatory term would be quite misleading. He certainly moved into the world of administration and government policy but for him it was a unique platform from which to exert influence and innovation. A part of his unique achievement is that without ever having the formal time to reflect and write, he produced a significant body of influential work that was significant well beyond his immediate domain of Australia. He was also instrumental in working with colleagues around the world to disseminate ideas that transcended national limitations.

As Bill Green demonstrates, this was partly because he was such an important presence, and 'presence' with Boomer is a key term, especially as a keynote speaker but essentially at any gathering of educators or politicians. Much of his best work began as a talk, a presentation, an address, and he would reveal new ideas and the prospects of significant change to a real audience who heard it there first, always leaving a powerful impression, and subsequently those ideas were written up, very often in essay format, and so later reached a wider audience through journal articles and edited volumes.

We move to the third circle which is that of international influence. Bill Green considers Boomer's very definite Australian character as part of his reflection on his distinctiveness, and that was a strength, never a limitation. Boomer was living at a time when he had to travel to make those impressive presentations and he was invited and celebrated all over the globe. He found time not only to attend many key events in the field of English teaching around the world but also to be active in developing international links and associations such as The International Federation for the Teaching of English. He also had a brief but very formative spell in London where he was strongly influenced by some other key thinkers from the field like James Britton, Harold Rosen, Nancy Martin, Douglas Barnes, just to mention a few. He essentially became their international colleague and later became acquainted with a number of significant thinkers from the USA and other countries – Bill Green explores all these influences in the volume. Garth Boomer was a remarkable Australian educator and a truly international and key figure in the history of English in education and the language arts.

Andy Goodwyn, February 2024

Preface

This book is intended as an introduction to and an outline of the work and career of Garth Boomer, a key figure in English curriculum history in Australia, and also the international English teaching field. As such, it is aimed ultimately at those working in English teaching in the 21st century – the present-day generations who constitute the field and the profession now and since his untimely death in the early 1990s. It is also intended as a historical account of what remains a key moment in that field. I argue here that Boomer's thinking about English teaching and the language arts continues to be relevant to current issues and challenges in curriculum and schooling more generally. But he is even more relevant in the context of the project of this larger series of monographs that invite us to look again at the leading ideas and figures associated with what I describe as 'post-Dartmouth English' – sometimes alternatively labelled the 'New English' – and to re-call them into play. Garth Boomer is clearly located within this tradition: he was an important figure within it, and he should be re-read accordingly. This book is intended as a resource in this regard, as well as being both a provocation and an invitation to do so. So who was he, and why is he important in such a context?

In the chapters that follow, I firstly seek to introduce and overview Boomer's work and career, providing what can here be only a biographical snapshot.[1] I move on to an account of the version of English teaching and subject English that he is associated with, which is organised discursively and historically around the Dartmouth Seminar, a celebrated transatlantic meeting of English educators from Britain and the USA, held in 1966. Biographical accounts generally focus on individuals, first and foremost, locating them in their life and times. The problem is that such an undertaking not only encourages a 'heroic' view of history, but it also perpetuates a certain ideology of the individual human(ist) subject. My challenge has been how this might be interrupted, and to what degree. While it is important to recognise, and acknowledge, particular figures as historical *agents*, as significant nodal points, there is indeed a danger in perpetuating a 'Great Man' view of educational history, perhaps especially so in cases like this. Yet Boomer worked with many others, constantly and consistently, and was emphatically collaborative.[2] He worked during the 1970s and 1980s. The 1970s, in particular, was a period of great social energy and renewal, spilling over into the next decade, despite major and decisive change, and persisting thereafter albeit sometimes subterraneously. It is this period that I focus on here, then.

In this 'biography' of a curriculum movement and moreover a *project*, the focus is not only on Boomer himself, as an individual educator, and a key figure in the field, but also on the larger context of social life and educational thought in that period. The book overviews Boomer's life and his career – cut short by his premature death at 52. It indicates the various roles he played – English teacher, English consultant, source-book writer, Superintendent, Chair of the National Curriculum Development Centre and the Australian Schools Commission, and Associate Director-General (Curriculum) in his home state of South Australia. But the book mainly focuses on the nature and significance of his *curriculum* thinking – hence its designation as a 'curriculum biography': a curriculum-biographical account of, in particular, key ideas in English teaching and related areas – specifically Boomer's arguments and provocations regarding English teaching, the English classroom, and the nested contexts that infuse and shape them.

Hence, this account also provides a contextualising curriculum history of the 1970s and 1980s, around the 'New English' and subsequently the 'New Right' backlash of the 1980s and the first emergent signs of neoliberalism. While the 1980s was heralded at its outset as the so-called "decade of the teacher" (Britton, 1982), hindsight highlights the cruel irony in such a pronouncement, with teachers and teaching in the following decades becoming more and more constrained and regulated across the English teaching world. Yet, even now, there are still important insights and challenges in Boomer's work and career that point to rich possibilities in the field for today and tomorrow. Operating as he did strategically, working with *and* against the grain of prevailing policy agendas, these possibilities might well be seized upon and seen as a powerful demonstration of English teaching as both pragmatic-intellectual practice and organic professionalism.

Central to this is Boomer's insistence on the importance of learners and learning – constituting therefore both a continuation and a renewal of perspectives and traditions associated historically with Dartmouth and the London School. Relatedly, his explorations of pedagogy in the context of new emphases on the crucial relationship between language and learning, culture and politics, experience and history, include his continued concern with what is called here 'teacher power'. In this sense I give due consideration to what is perhaps his signature concept: the notion of 'negotiating the curriculum', which is presented as a distinctive curriculum orientation, and hence a contribution to curriculum inquiry more generally.

A further matter addressed here, therefore, is the notion of *curriculum leadership*. This is understood firstly with reference to Boomer's own curriculum leadership, his practice, particularly with regard to English teaching and literacy education. More broadly and more generally, though, the record shows he was clearly a leader for the curriculum field in a range of other manifestations. I want to register his particular significance in terms of the relationship between English teaching and curriculum inquiry, and thus to bring to the fore something all too often overlooked in much English teaching professional and scholarly debate, which can at times be rather insular and inward-looking. As an English teacher, Boomer himself was markedly concerned with the *whole* school curriculum, and specifically with language-and-learning across the curriculum, and he was increasingly aware of contexts other than the English classroom *per se*, always understanding that the 'outside' was dynamically interwoven with the 'inside'. Hence the important work on language and literacy across the curriculum has meant that, in practice, English teaching has often been influential (sometimes to the point and at the risk of being accused of 'imperialism'…). So, accounting for curriculum leadership here is a way of acknowledging Boomer's exemplary role in setting agendas and constructing constituencies, as well as in promoting a view of English teaching as curriculum praxis, and also a form of curriculum leadership.

***

I want to strike a more personal note at this point. This has been a particularly difficult book to write. They all are, of course – for me, at least – but there has been something about this one that has troubled and challenged me right from the outset. It is only relatively recently that I realised what it was: the difficulty of understanding the relationship between Garth Boomer and myself; the difficulty, if not the impossibility, of disentangling the two of us, now, 30 years after his death in 1993, with me – just about to turn 72 – being almost 20 years older than he was when he died. For a time I even tried to avoid using the first-person and to keep myself out of the picture, as much as possible. But that proved to be a sure-fire way of creating a significant case of writer's block! It is still an issue for me, however. How to *write* such an account? How faithful is this representation of Garth Boomer to the historical reality? – to other people's experiences and memories of him, while he was alive. Need it be? He has become to some extent mythologised, and institutionalised in various ways – for instance, there are annual keynote lectures presented each year in Australia at national conferences which are named after him. And, as part of my use of the first-person narrative voice here, my struggle has been to maintain a certain balance – are these Boomer's ideas, or are they mine? Or, much more likely, is it rather a productive mix of the two of us, 'scholar' and 'practitioner', in dialogue. For instance: Is this a more politicised Garth Boomer than was the actual case – although certainly he was politically very savvy. But was he engaging theory, and bringing a theoretical rigour to his political thinking and his praxis, as suggested here? I think he was – and I must say, I'm all the more convinced of this, now having worked through the writing of this book. Moreover, a key principle he thoroughly endorsed is that ideas are always collective, communal – moreover, "[g]ood ideas prevail and grow" (Boomer, 1988a, p. 237). And he had plenty of good ideas…

Moreover, there are so many Garth Boomers out there, in people's heads, mine included – he was an early inspiration and mentor and later a good friend, and a major influence on my ongoing work. As well as that, however, I have edited two volumes of his essays, and a special issue in his memory (2013) of the journal *English in Australia* – and there are a range of references to his work across various writings of my own (e.g., Green, 2018a). So there are various accounts that could have been written, with differing orientations and emphases, and still might be. This version of Garth here is distinctive, I suggest, in that it is based to a significant extent on the *texts*, on the archive of the papers he produced across much of his professional and intellectual career. The status of these papers is somewhat unclear: many are of an informal nature; some are official documents of various kinds; and many are effectively drafts towards later, more formal presentations and publications. My own editorial work in this regard is relevant here – especially with the books of his essays. In putting them together I tended to take a more active editorial role, which in some instances constituted a form of curatorship – to the point of re-contextualising, assembling text, etc. Finally, I believe that my own theoretical/conceptual work, not just with regard to English teaching but in curriculum theory and curriculum inquiry more generally, clearly reveals his influence. Even though I acknowledge that, as individuals, we have worked in very different ways and registers, I continue to learn from him, even now, and writing this book has proved very generative in that regard.

Despite my disclaimers here, though, something needs to be said about the man himself, as variously recalled by those who knew him and worked with him. There were a number of commentaries when he died, as might be expected, and they strike a consistent note, highlighting an exuberant personality who enjoyed his life and his work, and who especially valued the company of others. These ranged from tributes from old friends like Peter MacFarlane (1993) and Claire Woods (1993), both fellow South Australians, to celebrations elsewhere such as from John Mayher and Nancy Lester (1993) in the American journal *English Education*. Paul Brock, another Australian, later recalled these in his 2013 account of Boomer's work and life, noting in particular Mayher and Lester's "vividly recognisable portrait of Garth: raconteur; scholar; derring-do; gastronome; bon vivant; connoisseur and imbiber of quality red wine; scallywag; singer and dancer; lover of literature; proud Aussie" (Brock, 2013, p. 20). Mayher himself, 20 years on from Boomer's passing in 1993, wrote powerfully of Boomer's impact, not just on himself but on English teaching more generally, including in the States – even as he acknowledged that it has been hard going in that country for what is called here post-Dartmouth English teaching. As for Boomer's influence, he suggested, this was a matter as much as anything else of *presence*. Boomer was undoubtedly a large personality. As Mayher (2013, p. 21) wrote:

> [GB] was passionately committed to the work and loved to talk about it, but he was by no means a dull workaholic – he loved to sing and dance and above all to laugh. He told funny stories and consistently saw the absurdity in the pompous and stuffy people inside and out of our profession. And he was consistently generous: seeking to support good ideas and strong voices wherever he could find them.

I too have engaged in this kind of commentary, but I've always felt that Boomer himself was wary of how this all too often played out. Hence his reflexivity, his willingness to turn the critical gaze back on himself, to catch himself out. This is captured neatly in the following:

> In my own teaching these days, I deliberately seek to alienate my students from my teaching performance by showing them what I am about. I wish to

rouse their suspicions about what I say and do, so that I will be tested before swallowing. *I always try to teach the meta-text along with the text.*

(Boomer, 1988k, p. 66; my added emphasis)

It is in contexts such as this that he introduced the notion, and the pedagogy and politics, of *interruption*. But this was done, more often than not, in a spirit of fun, of irreverence. His were *lasting* lessons, yes, but they were also what I call here *larrikin* lessons, which is a theme or perhaps a motif that I hope permeates this book – reminding us, once again, to remember what it's all about and what it's for, and to take the opportunity, whenever, to have a laugh. I've always been impressed by Donald Macedo's (1985, pp. 195–198) wonderful portrait of Paulo Freire in informal company, having a meal with friends, sharing a drink, joking, talking… Garth Boomer was like that. He enjoyed company and conversation. He appreciated a fine wine and he loved a good beer. He *lived* life.

Something I wrote once comes to mind, and still seems apposite: "Garth Boomer was an English teacher, first and foremost – an English teacher and a teacher of English teachers. That is, he was a *teacher* and he was a teacher of *English*" (Green, 2003a, p. 1). As I continued: "He loved words, language, the play of sentences and sayings, the unruly metaphor, the dazzling dancing image". All that still rings true for me, two decades on. He enjoyed the wor(l)d, and he loved to watch it turn. But he was very serious about education and public schooling and much else, all the same. This is someone who could write "[e]very new thought is the seed for a possible story", and also mourn how story was being stripped so systematically from curriculum. He was an agent provocateur. He was all of that, and more. He lived a rich and rewarding life, even though he had his struggles along the way, and he had his critics, as I touch on in this book.

I've been shocked, I must say, by the poverty of our historical imagination, as English educators. Being aware of Boomer, his work, his legacy, is a good example of this: how many of those entering the field and the profession in recent times have any real sense of who he was and why he matters? Or is that simply the way of things, same as it ever was? Maybe. Garth Boomer remains, undoubtedly, a key figure in English teaching and the language arts, and I hope that the book that follows does justice to his ideas and insights, and his contribution not just to our thinking and our practice, but also to our resilience and courage, as a resource, in and for what are certainly difficult and challenging times.

Notes

1 See Reid (2017). Boomer's contribution to curriculum inquiry, certainly in Australia, merits extended consideration in its own right – it is only touched on here, and mostly in specific relation to English teaching and literacy education.
2 This is nicely put by one of his long-time colleagues in the South Australian education department, in acknowledging Boomer's leadership and vision over four decades, and his "energy, direction and thinking": "He did not work alone, he relied on others to provide structure, management, motivation and thinking, but his vision and willingness to confront old thinking and ways, was the driver of change" (Dellit, 2011, p. 154).

Acknowledgements

A number of people provided important and timely advice and/or support along the way. I would like to especially acknowledge Phil Cormack, Marie Brennan, Wayne Sawyer, and Lucinda McKnight.

I also want to thank Andy Goodwyn for his patience, and for taking on what might have seemed a rather risky project early on.

Kerry Mahony was extremely helpful in formatting the manuscript, and also assisting with the index.

Jo-Anne Reid continues to be my most important supporter, and my partner in everything that counts. Her extensive, detailed assistance and unwavering confidence that this was something worth doing, and that I could indeed get it done, is greatly appreciated, as always. Her work on the index is especially acknowledged.

1 Introduction and Overview

Garth Boomer – Teacher, Writer, Intellectual

Garth Boomer (1940–1993) was a leading figure in English teaching in Australia, working in the key period of the 1970s and 1980s, extending into the early 1990s. He died in 1993, aged 52. This book constitutes an introduction to his work, with particular focus on English curriculum and teaching. In doing so, it also engages various matters pertaining to literacy education, teacher development, curriculum inquiry, and educational policy, with specific regard to Australia but also taking due account of his influence overseas. His professional leadership is indicated by the fact that, as well as serving as President of the Australian Association for the Teaching of English (AATE), he was also President of the International Federation of Teachers of English (IFTE). Highly sought after as a charismatic and compelling conference speaker, his publications included books of essays on English teaching and literacy education, as well as practical source-books for the classroom teaching of secondary English.

An Australian educator who was clearly the foremost figure in English teaching in Australia in the 1970s and 1980s, and arguably one of the leading English educators of the period right across the English-teaching world, Garth Boomer could not be characterised as an academic or a conventional 'scholar', at least in the commonly recognised sense. He worked throughout his career as a teacher and a bureaucrat, employed within education systems and state offices. He never worked in universities, or in formal teacher education. As he noted, somewhat archly:

> By 1982, the English teacher was undergoing metamorphosis. His career had taken him away from English into the broader field of curriculum development and in-service education. It was a logical progression because talking language inevitably leads one to consider learning, and learning is at the heart of all education.
>
> (Boomer, 1985a, p. 153)

A prolific writer, his publications were often first and foremost texts prepared for conferences and professional gatherings, of various magnitudes, for presentation and performance and hence rhetorical re-working. While some of these texts

DOI: 10.4324/9781003374886-1

subsequently appeared in academic and professional outlets, they might be read sometimes as 'thin', especially from a more elite academic perspective that fails to recognise them for what they were – performance texts and rhetoric, and hence always already invoking and involving an Other.

The key point is that his work differs from the usual academic-intellectual exposition – the scholarly paper. What must be remembered, too, is that Boomer characteristically composed, and thought, *across* texts more often than not, on the run so to speak, and hence his ideas and arguments tend to be realised not so much in depth as horizontally, in what has been called a "rhetoric of surfaces" (Green & Meiers, 2003). A particular idea or rather an *image* might be re-worked and rehearsed across various occasions and forums before emerging in a key presentation or paper as a fully developed formulation. This is extremely significant in coming to Boomer's 'writing', his written work from that time – the only basis now, in fact, for accessing and engaging his 'curriculum thinking'. As we assess his historical and intellectual significance, it is important to understand that so much of this published work was originally presented as 'speeches', at specific conference events. The focus was on the occasion: *this* audience, *here* and *now* – *how* he was addressing them, and *why*. As ideas and arguments are developed across texts, rather than worked up in detail or elaborated in any one occasion, they are thus 'tested out', and evolve, more or less experimentally.

Boomer himself talked about this in his introduction to a collection of his early essays:

> When I write occasional pieces such as these, I hear my voice delivering the words and I imagine the dramatic tensions which will be built between me and my audience. The challenge is not to be as concise and as precise as possible, but to cast out related networks of meaning which, cumulatively or retrospectively, will make connections with most of the listeners and generate some understanding of some of the ideas I wish to spread.
>
> (Boomer, 1988b, p. 1)

He was thus aiming for a contagion-effect, "a kind of infectiousness" (p. 1) – something that might now be thought about in terms of affect theory. It is not surprising, therefore, that his work is available mainly in edited books and similar fora, and generally speaking scattered about in fugitive contexts. Boomer typically worked up the conference keynote as a *pedagogic* opportunity; and the links between pedagogy and rhetoric are well worth acknowledging here. Metaphor is crucial, as he noted elsewhere: "The more richly the teacher can spin a tapestry of metaphor and analogy into a 'thick' redundant text of thinking about something new, the more likely it is that students will find a way in" (Boomer, 1982a, p. 120). His own writing demonstrates this as at once a rhetorical and a pedagogic strategy.

He readily acknowledged the costs and dangers of such an approach: "My writing, abstracted from the occasion, will tend to frustrate readers who treat it according to the conventional genre of academic essay or journal article. *It is not of that genre*" (Boomer, 1988a, p. 2; my added emphasis). "I rely on considerable charges of affectivity", he wrote: "I do not want cool appraisal. I want images to work as powerfully as arguments" (p. 2). The problem is, history works only with written records, with 'writing', and with audio-visual documents when those are available, which means that work such as Boomer's must be supplemented and relayed by the writing of others, as is my own challenge here.

A Scholar-Practitioner

In this regard, Boomer belongs on the 'teacher' side of the Dartmouth divide that Joseph Harris (2012) and other commentators (e.g., Durst, 2015) talk about. "[R]ather than the scene of a heroic shift in the theory and practice of [English] teaching", Dartmouth staged the conflicts inherent in the field "with unusual clarity", Harris (2012, p. 4) writes. These were particularly apparent between the values and perspectives of the British and American contingents. In this regard, "if the American hero was the scholar, then the British hero was the teacher" (p. 3). This tension between the 'scholars' and the 'teachers', the 'theorists' and the 'practitioners', remains evident today, even though it would now be readily conceded that there are representatives of both camps on each side of the divide. Boomer would clearly be identified from this perspective with the 'teachers' – and yet as I contend here, his intellectual contribution and scholarly significance is just as emphatic. Writing on James Britton's 'anti-disciplinary' stance, Durst (2015) has pointed to "ongoing tensions in the field between pedagogy and scholarship" (p. 385), suggesting that Britton may best be seen as a 'scholar-practitioner', citing Tirrell (1990) in this regard.[1] This is to be understood from a distinctly American point of view, it would seem, given what Durst implies is the apparent priority in American institutional life of scholarship over pedagogy. Boomer is also to be seen as similarly a scholar-practitioner, then – with the proviso that this is not seen in such culturally constrained terms but, rather, as a distinctive style and ethos, consistent with a strong post-Dartmouth tradition in praxis and inquiry, with its own positivity and productivity. Indeed there is a particular case to be argued that Boomer is best regarded as a 'scholar-practitioner' *par excellence*, in his case practising both as an educator and as a bureaucrat, as an administrative intellectual, engaged in the practical politics of large education systems. Durst proposes "doubling down on pedagogy" (p. 398), and this is precisely what Boomer did, imbuing it with his own sense of scholarship (and that of others), while embracing what he was later to describe as "a new pragmatic-radical intellectualism in the teaching profession" (Boomer, 1999a, p. 124).

A key figure not only nationally but internationally, then, Boomer was instrumental in what might be described as the second major phase of the 'New English', in the 1970s and 1980s. The 'New English' curriculum formation emerged from the 1966 Dartmouth Seminar, and became a dominant paradigm in the field, especially in Australia, New Zealand, (Anglophone) Canada, and the United Kingdom, although perhaps less so in the USA. Boomer (re)presented a distinctive vision of English teaching (post-Dartmouth), pushing the field into new territory with respect to curriculum inquiry and professional education. At the same time, he continued to engage in serious conceptualisation of the key organising principle(s) of language and learning, increasingly understood with explicit reference to power and politics. Rhetorician, passionate advocate, and larrikin[2] – notwithstanding the fact that he became a senior educational bureaucrat – he remained deeply committed to classroom practice and its associated policy contexts and constraints throughout his whole career. As I argued above, he clearly exemplifies the New English tradition of the scholar-practitioner.

Moreover, although distinctively Australian, his work has remained enduringly of international interest and relevance. But it is interesting, all the same, to consider what happens to theory and pedagogy when it travels across contexts, borders, and traditions. The theory travelled literally, in Boomer's case, from England to Australia initially – and subsequently he of course travelled to London. Australian English teachers studying in England came under the influence of ideas originally nurtured in inner London. As I describe below, these were developed there and elsewhere within the empire of English, and a new transnational professional conversation opened up. What was it that so informed and energised Garth Boomer that he devoted his life to English teaching and curriculum leadership, in a way that continues to inspire today?

English Teaching Post-Dartmouth – or, Professing the New English?

Boomer described "the years 1972–1973" as "a watershed in [his] career". As he wrote:

> These were the years which I spent in study at the English as Mother-Tongue Department of the University of London, Institute of Education, looking in particular at how teachers learn, with a specific focus on teachers within an English department at an inner London school. The study came after ten years of work as an English teacher and consultant with the Education Department of South Australia.
>
> (Boomer, 1988b, pp. 1–2)

This was clearly a momentous period for him, personally as well as professionally. But it was so for the wider field too. The London Writing Project was in full flight. Britton's *Language and Learning* had been published in 1970, and just the year before, *Language, the Learner and the School* (Barnes et al., 1969) had erupted on the scene, with a revised edition emerging in 1971. *The Development of Writing Abilities (11–18)* was to appear in 1975. Boomer worked directly with Nancy Martin and Harold Rosen, whom he described as "my chief supervisors, teachers and critics" (p. 3), though there can be no doubt that he interacted widely and made important and enduring connections with many at the Institute and beyond.

It needs to be recalled, too, that this was also the time of *Knowledge and Control* (Young, 1971), which ushered in the new sociology of education, and heralded an escalating turn to social analysis and a new political awareness in education and schooling. Basil Bernstein in particular became a point of fascination, as well as cultural scholars such as Raymond Williams. So 'London' was a crucial reference-point for Boomer, clearly – what became known as the 'London School', originally as formulated by Stephen Ball (1985), although this was always used rhetorically and strategically, and suffused with other 'Schools' ('Cambridge', 'Birmingham', 'Sydney') in English curriculum-historical scholarship (e.g., Green, 1995a, 1995b). It was also directly connected with John Dixon's *Growth Through English*, first published as a report on the famous Dartmouth transatlantic seminar, held in 1966, and with a revised edition in 1975 – hence the so-called 'Growth Model'.

So both 'London' and 'Dartmouth' are keywords here, in introducing and reviewing Boomer's work and its significance, marking out the discursive field within which he operated – and it is important to discuss them here, to some extent, as a crucial context for this account. Much has been written about both, of course, embracing the full range from celebration and elaboration to criticism and critique. Yet they risk becoming myth, and need to be reanimated and brought alive again and again, for different generations, as Derrida reminds us so beautifully, albeit referring himself to philosophy:

> [W]hoever inherits chooses one spirit or another. One makes selections, one filters through the ghosts or through the injunctions of each spirit. There is legacy only where assignations are multiple and contradictory, secret enough to defy interpretation, to carry the unlimited risk of active interpretation.
> (Derrida, 2002, p. 111; cited in Egéa-Kuehne, 2003, pp. 273–274)

What then is the 'legacy' associated with London and Dartmouth, in the discourse of English teaching? How are we to manage the ghosts that circulate in the ether around us, and what is it that we have inherited? My sense is that, while Boomer was keenly aware of working in a 'living' tradition, of living (in) history, it is only when he himself is actively (re)drawn into professional memory, as here, that the enduring value of his work becomes apparent.

Perhaps the single most distinguishing feature of what can be called post-Dartmouth English teaching, in its strongest version, is appropriately summarised in the formulation 'language and learning'. That is, a new emphasis was placed on both language and learning, in themselves, *and* the relationship between them. It is all too easy now to underplay the significance of this shift in emphasis. Emerging from it was a re-worked understanding of English teaching, filtered through a process-developmental view of language and education. It is this version that I think warrants being described as the primary discourse of post-Dartmouth English teaching, by which I mean the strongest and most significant, and enduring – the one that matters most, educationally, ethically and politically. This claim cannot be simply presumed, or pre-ordained, of course; rather, it needs to be reinvented, in and for each and every circumstance and generation, and supplemented appropriately. Indeed, it can be argued that its meaning-potential remains even now to be fully actualised. Part of the issue here, in my view, is that the field and its governing scholarship moved on too quickly, without also doing the work required to properly excavate and interrogate what already existed. Another part of the issue involved here, then, is drawing in other bodies of work making aligned arguments, some of which have only become available subsequently, for example the 'funds of knowledge' work (Moll, 2014) which shares all the basic premises and implications of language and learning theory, and *making* the connections.

On Language and Learning

The notion of 'language and learning' is a deceptively simple formulation which nonetheless is of great and lasting import, pointing as it does to a crucial move in the discourse on English teaching post-Dartmouth. This might even be described as subject English's own 'linguistic turn', echoing and paralleling a broader shift in the human sciences at the time. This was the moment when a new awareness of language emerged on the scene and quickly took centre-stage. A new view of the relationship between language and thought was at issue here, signalled as much as anything else in the rise into prominence of the Russian psychologist and scholar Vygotsky. Language was now to be seen as crucial in and for learning, properly conceived. It was instrumental in human learning, and formative, in important and distinctive ways. At the same time, it directly suggested a new focus on *learning* itself, a new understanding, one involving a shift to a 'process' view – learning as a *process*. This was opposed to a longstanding emphasis on learning as substantive, as a *thing*. Similarly, language was seen as not so much an object, in and of itself, but as an activity, and a practice in its own right, a process occurring in time and moreover realising and registering change, a transformation. Teaching, therefore, involved a process-development view of language and learning alike. Perhaps one of the most effective ways of conveying what this involved was in the formulation: 'from information to understanding'. That is, learning is not simply a matter of engaging *information*, rather this needed to be realised anew, as *understanding*[3] – in Bakhtinian terms, it needed to become "internally persuasive". (This also meant, of course, a different and distinctive view of knowledge.) Both language and learning were thereby reconceptualised, as was the relationship between them.

Working from within the London tradition, John Hardcastle has provided an insightful account of how this reformulated view of language and learning can be traced back to the European Enlightenment. His focus is "the role of signs in the formation of mind" (Hardcastle, 2009). Drawing on such notable figures such as Condillac, Herder, and von Humboldt, he stresses the role that signification plays in the emergence of "specifically human consciousness" (p. 188), "the active expression of reflective consciousness" (Hardcastle, 1997, p. 33), and hence what might be called the post-Cartesian construction of subjectivity. While he links all this to Vygotsky, noting in particular "the influence of the Humboldt tradition on Vygotsky's thought" (Hardcastle, 2009, p. 183), he stops short, here, in connecting more broadly to Russian linguistic scholarship and to Marxist views of language.[4] However, the contextualisation of post-Dartmouth English teaching and the London School in terms of Enlightenment thought is important, laying out its larger history. Britton himself drew directly on Ernst Cassirer and Suzanne

Langer, among others (e.g., Gusdorf, 1965), in his work, most notably his signature book *Language and Learning* (1970). This is an intellectual aspect of the tradition that is all too often overlooked, or underestimated: the significance of the philosophy of language.

What all this translated into, in classroom practice, was a new emphasis on learners and learning in English teaching, and on experience and activity and interest[5] as key principles. Classrooms were increasingly organised with a focus on language as a means and resource for learning. This was a major shift away from traditional classroom organisation and interaction: it involved teachers organising students to engage in exploratory talk and writing (talking to learn); it involved students working on 'real' writing (i.e., purposeful writing for authentic audiences), on narrative and poetry, on interaction and exchange, on dialogue. In Britton's terms, 'expressive' and 'poetic' functions of language became increasingly central, particularly with regard to subject English, with a somewhat different emphasis on the 'transactional': "As English teachers we have more and more come to see our responsibility as focusing upon the spectrum of language usage from the expressive to the poetic – language, in other words, in the role of spectator" (Britton, 1973, p. 25). While this formulation was to become increasingly problematical, for many, even so it has been generative, overall, especially in encouraging inquiry into the specificity of subject English in the school curriculum. (This latter issue is taken up in Chapter 4.) Importantly, and enduringly, the expressive function in language usage was seen as "a kind of matrix, a starting-point from which the other two develop" (p. 24) – at the heart of the process-developmental perspective, as outlined above. Not at all unrelatedly, these shifts meant there was a growing emphasis on teachers' engagement, agency, and activism, on 'becoming our own experts' and working collaboratively with other teachers, not only in English departments[6] but beyond, in and across the profession. That activism in some cases became more political in nature, and so different orientations emerged, with a child-centred liberal 'progressivism' on one side and a more socially critical perspective on the other – both however with a programmatic acknowledgement of the value of students' lives, cultures, and identities – and with frequent overlaps between the two.

Boomer was deeply immersed in and clearly committed to this emerging view of English teaching. As he writes in an early paper, "our stance was at first unequivocally British" (Boomer, 1973, p. 75), although there were later moves towards greater and more explicit engagement with North American influences, initially and notably the work of James Moffett. At the same, as Boomer pointed out on various occasions, there was much in the post-1960s Australian scene that was already receptive to such thinking, with "its own distinctive personalities at the cutting edge of the advance" (p. 75). Moreover, "most of them [were] teachers or at least closely involved with the practicalities of teaching" (p. 75). This is much akin to what Peter Medway and his colleagues documented in post-war London schools, in the 'pre-history' of New English (Medway et al., 2014). Boomer himself became a key figure in this respect, first in his home state of South Australia and then nationally, participating in, developing, and leading major initiatives in language and learning, more often than not under state-systemic auspices. He was thoroughly committed to the new curriculum theories and frameworks, however, and the crucial significance of language in education, and remained so throughout his career, yet he was always strategic in this regard, when his work was aimed at teacher change. This can be seen in his signature statement on 'negotiating the curriculum', first published in 1978 (Boomer, 1992a).[7] Specifically acknowledging Britton's influence here, he proposed asking the question 'How do children (and for that matter, we) learn?' prior to asking 'How do children learn language?' – that is, he sought to place a strategic focus on *learning* rather than language, in part because he was dealing with participant-practitioners beyond subject English. This didn't mean downplaying or glossing over language, though, and considerable effort went into arguing for and exploring how language works in and for learning, all across the curriculum. Language ('language-ing') in fact was crucial to the personal-practical 'learning theories' that he advocated teachers needed to develop *for themselves* (Boomer, 1992a, p. 5). This was the basis for envisioning teachers as what he early on described as "active campaigners" (Boomer, 1973, p. 66) and later as "pragmatic radicals" (Boomer, 1999b), something dealt with here in Chapter 3.

Pedagogy, Imagination, Creativity

This focus on teachers, and teachers learning, led to Boomer becoming increasingly interested in the then-unfashionable notion of *pedagogy*. He began to talk more and more about the 'art and science' of pedagogy, although this was sometimes expressed as 'the art and science of teaching'. Again, it was the relationship between teaching and learning that he was concerned with – the teacher's use of language and its effects on how students learn, or 'come to know'. To refer to teachers' work as 'teaching', as traditionally the case, might not allow proper emphasis on and acknowledgement of that relationship. 'Pedagogy' as a concept brought together teaching and learning. And it required reflection on how best to describe and to understand the nature of that relationship. Which had priority – teaching or learning? Can one be achieved without the other? Thus was ushered in what can now be seen as the paradox of pedagogy – pedagogy *as* paradox – that is central to appreciating Boomer's overall project. Moreover, that paradox, I propose, is at the very heart of post-Dartmouth English teaching. If learning was indeed a new organising principle, what did that mean for teaching? Particularly for teaching the New English? This is partly what is at issue in some of the views held by people inside and outside the field, for whom subject English, post-1960s, had become "unintelligible" (Medway, 1990a), unrecognisable, even ungrammatical, and seemingly counter-normative. The terms could be extended: strange, different, deviant, etc. This was the New as monster, as monstrosity (cf. Derrida, 1978, p. 293). Whatever the case, a powerful, even visceral reaction followed in the media and the wider society, with the demonising of 'progressivism' and new demands for the restoration of pedagogic authority – for reinstalling the figure of the Teacher (Green, 1998). And what must be pointed to as a primary catalyst in this regard is the *paradox of pedagogy* in the new post-Dartmouth dispensation: the new relationship envisaged between teaching and learning, teachers and learners. Britton (1973) had eloquently expressed this early on, in fact, in his characteristically modest way: "I have shared in a movement towards a conception of learning that gives quite a different meaning to teaching" (p. 15).[8] Much subsequent effort went into working out this new relationship in practice and in classrooms, across the English teaching world. Boomer is an important reference-point in this regard, increasingly seeking to articulate the nature of pedagogy, and to indicate, in particular, what this meant for teachers and teaching (cf. Green, 2003a).

His thinking and writing moved easily, organically, between learning and teaching, teaching and learning.[9] As he writes, in his early manifesto:

> By reflecting on what it is that human beings do when they learn, it is possible to arrive at principles of learning, which can then be transformed into principles of teaching. Practice based on these principles focuses in the first place on *what the learner is doing* and only secondarily on *what the teacher must do.*
> (Boomer, 1982b, p. viii)

This is much akin to Britton's formulation above, just as emphatic but also caught up in a similarly restricted logic (this... and then that...). The two need to be brought together, however, at least conceptually – teaching AND learning – but perhaps also rhetorically, or grammatically, however difficult or even impossible that seems to be. Even so, there is surely evidence here of Boomer struggling in his expression with this very problem ('what the learner is doing', 'what the teacher must do'). Furthermore, for Boomer, crucially, learning itself properly conceived involves creativity and imagination. As he wrote: "Imagination is at the heart of learning" (Boomer, 1999c, p. 15). Further:

> Imagination is what differentiates human beings from the rest of the animal world. We are able to hold images in our heads and think about them in the same way that we think about the real world. And so, imagination frees us from the tyranny of the here-and-now. It allows us to go back into the past and forward into possible futures. Through imagination, we can be where we are physically not. Imagination is the Tardis of humankind.
> (p. 15)

Moreover, "[f]or those of us who work in schools", as he puts it, "imagination is the high-octane fuel of learning" (p. 15). This requires that teachers, in seeking to promote powerful learning, "must know how to stir imaginations, to excite a search for possibilities, and to encourage reflection and imaginative hindsight" (p. 15).

Similarly, with regard to creativity: Boomer saw learning as necessarily creative, as making meaning – or rather, *making meaning matter*. He described creativity as "a quality or attribute which has at its core the power of making things", adding to this "for a purpose" and linking it to particular notions of 'intention' and 'design' (Boomer, 1987a, p. 119). He saw creativity as 'ordinary', and as deeply associated with living and learning. Creativity should be understood across a spectrum, encompassing "making things up – making believe – playing", "making things happen – acting" and "making things – making things work – engineering" (Boomer, 1987a, pp. 120–122). Creativity, as he summarises, "pertains to acts of making: making believe, making things happen and making things for a purpose" (p. 122). The links with how learning is being (re)conceptualised above, moving from information to understanding and into action, are clear.

My point here is that Boomer had indeed a rich and robust view of learning – student learning, but also teacher learning – and this is indicated as much as anything in his emphasis on *metaphor*, which he saw as central to language and learning, and to pedagogy. "The more richly the teacher can spin a tapestry of metaphor and analogy into a 'thick' redundant text of thinking about something new, the more likely it is that students will find a way in" (Boomer, 1982a, p. 120). There are important connections to be made between his work in this regard and that of Vygotsky, especially the latter's emphasis on affect, imagination and creativity, and the role and significance of art (Barrs, 2021). Teaching needs to emphasise thinking *and* feeling, across the full range of language and learning: "In order to create, we design, concentrate, speculate, observe, theorise, indwell, recall, combine and connect, explore, predict, anticipate, apply, test, evaluate, and appreciate; that is, we think and feel" (Boomer, 1987a, p. 123).

This meant that for pedagogy, then, imagination is crucial, as Boomer consistently argued:

> The teacher must indwell in the problem of the learner and be able to recreate in his or her own mind the thoughts and feelings of one who is coming to this territory for the first time.
>
> (Boomer, 1988c, p. 177)

Indeed, this can appropriately be called the pedagogical imagination, or, as it is described elsewhere, the imagination of otherness (Green, 2003a). The teacher images and imagines the learner, learning. We put ourselves in the learner's shoes, we look out from their eyes. We act 'as if' – and we do that as much in Graduate School as in Year 8, or Grade 3. What is it like for them (each one of them, in all their differences), coming to this particular (learning) territory for the first time? It's an act of double imagination, in fact – of imagining twice-over: what it is like to learn *that*, and what it is like *for them*, learning. How is such an imagination to be cultivated? – that's precisely the challenge. It has an inescapable ethical dimension too: imagining the other is always ethically charged, and this is quite specific in education and schooling. Is it *possible* to do the task fully? It is worth recalling Britton's invocation of Bernstein in the concluding words of *Language and Learning*'s Chapter 4 ('Now You Go to School'): "if the culture of the teacher is to become part of the consciousness of the child, then the culture of the child must first be in the consciousness of the teacher" (Britton, 1970, p. 188). This is certainly a sociological and political point, but it is inevitably ethical as well, and this is clearly realised in the exchanges and encounters of

English in Australia

Notwithstanding the relevance of the UK and the Dartmouth tradition, it is important to see Boomer's work in English teaching in the specific context of English in Australia. Although more clearly a national figure in English curriculum history, he has an international significance, over and beyond his own 'overseas' commitments and engagements. Moreover, the Australian scene is itself a key factor here. What happens to the New English, and more specifically the 'Growth' framework, as it travels and is re-contextualised around the world? Is English in Australia simply a more or less faithful version of an original or originating identity, or does it have distinctive features of its own, and its own transformed curriculum form? Boomer tackled this issue in an early paper when he referred to the way in which Australian English teachers were taking up the new ideas, marrying them with their own emerging practices and insights, and beginning to forge their own practical theories: "Australia is not 'making the best of both worlds' [i.e. England and America]; it is 'a bona fide partner in a world-wide movement, a burgeoning of life in the teaching of English" (Boomer, 1973, p. 67). This line of thinking clearly continued into the 1980s, and beyond, notably represented by the 1980 IFTE conference held in Sydney. Boomer's observation in 1973 that "quite clearly progressivism, if not radicalism, now dominates the national consciousness of English" (p. 67) can be matched by a later claim that "the International English Teachers' Conference in Sydney in 1980 … might arguably be seen as the high point of 'progressivism' or the 'new' English in Australia" (Kostogriz & Doecke, 2008; cf. Green & Sawyer, 2023). Australian figures have since continued to contribute significantly to the transnational discourse on English teaching and the language arts – for instance, with regard to literary education and reader-response pedagogy, 'critical literacy', and the genre movement in writing pedagogy and language education. Boomer (1985b, p. 189) himself took keynotes and other professional opportunities overseas as what he described as "a glorious chance to blow the Australian trumpet".[10]

An important consideration in this regard is the manner in which education and schooling is organised in Australia. The country comprises a federation of states and territories, each historically with primary responsibility for public education in their jurisdictions: more recently, the Commonwealth Government has increasingly exercised national oversight and taken on a formal regulative role tied to the provision of funding. Nonetheless, Australian education has tended to be state-centralised and bureaucratised, and still is, to a considerable degree.[11] What this has meant, in practice, is that the 'system' has always been influential in educational change and stability, and in either promoting or hindering reform. Boomer noted this feature and pointed to the fact, notwithstanding, that the late 60s and early 70s were marked by wider bureaucratic *support* for education innovation, with the 'system' "now becoming a powerful agent for change, growth and variety in education" (Boomer, 1973, p. 65; see also Boomer, 1999i). He was cognisant, accordingly, of how important government and systemic support was for educational policy and practice, and of the need to take due account therefore of prevailing structures and conditions, including appropriate infrastructure and its various affordances. His own later career was spent in educational bureaucracies, of one kind or another, and he remained keenly aware that such systemic framing had significant implications for what was possible in schools in the Australian context.

It is important to recognise the degree to which educational innovation and reform is constrained or enabled by government endorsement and support. Examples include the early official support in Australia for the New English, including the pioneering 1971 English Syllabus in New South Wales, which has been described as "the first official Growth syllabus in the world" (Sawyer, 2008); national initiatives like the Early Literacy Inservice Course in the 1980s; and later the nationwide take-up of 'critical literacy' in formal English curriculum policy (Luke, 2000). It is worth noting, further, that in Australia it has traditionally been senior bureaucrats and administrators rather than academics who have been the most influential figures in shaping curriculum discourse and the practice and character of schooling (Green, 1999, 2003b). Boomer's distinctive curriculum leadership is definitely to be viewed in this light.

Yet he was always an out-rider, indeed something of an outlaw, even as he came to occupy senior roles in the educational bureaucracy, working consistently and constantly as he did with *and* against the grain. This was part of his 'larrikin' image, but it was also central to his advocacy and his own project, in and beyond English teaching. It was also indicative of his characteristic reflexivity, his firm emphasis on the power and significance of (self-)reflection, on turning a critical eye back upon ourselves, as educators and as designers – which includes the 'designs' we have on others, notably our students. This would lead him, eventually, to explore a Brechtian perspective in his pedagogy and his curriculum thinking, to be elaborated later in Chapter 3. It also meant becoming caught, increasingly, in various misunderstandings, especially in the latter part of his career, when teachers were becoming resistant to increasingly conservative government change. Some saw him as 'selling out', while others viewed him with growing disappointment and even suspicion as 'part of the establishment'. This was something he was keenly aware of, and mourned.

The fact that he had always operated *inside* the system, at various levels, meant taking on different perspectives and working strategically, accordingly, with different stakeholders and constituencies. In a late paper, he reported some advice that Britton had offered him, a decade earlier, regarding "our greatest challenge over the next decade?": "You said, 'We need to learn how to make better and better compromises'" (Boomer, 1988a, p. 231). While rather sceptical at the time, Boomer could now see the wisdom of such advice, he said, including its strategic value, and indeed he acknowledged the connection to his own curriculum work.[12] Yet there are always costs to such compromises, and cumulatively, all the more so as the stakes rise. And this they did, clearly, over the 1980s, as the New Right came to dominance, before morphing into the neoliberalism that has shaped everything in the subsequent decades (Reid, 2019). More than most, perhaps, Boomer was located in the belly of the beast... Yet he remained consistent in his commitment to 'progressive' curriculum and schooling, and to English teachers and English teaching, and also to thinking and acting against the grain, speaking out and making trouble.

It is for this reason that he is widely regarded, still, as one of Australia's leading and most influential figures in English teaching, and in literacy education more generally. A recent keynote at the national conference of English teachers and literacy educators claims that:

> For those of us who entered the profession in the last decades of the 20th century, it would have been impossible to avoid the influence of Garth Boomer, such was the reach and magnitude of his personality, his ideas and his impact.
>
> (Manuel, 2023, p. 2)

Some did, undoubtedly, as we shall see later in this book, and there remains a certain degree of mythologisation in how and why he lives on today, as a spectral presence. This is all too often linked, in my own view, to the likelihood that he is rarely read in anything more than a fragmentary (or fragment-grabbing) manner, and certainly not with the rigour and seriousness his work warrants, taking due account of its intertextuality. Hopefully this book will provide guidance in this regard.

The Book: An Overview

The following chapters deal with different aspects of Boomer's work, specifically with regard to English and the language arts in education. The first, 'Negotiating the (English) Curriculum' (Chapter 2), is addressed to what is perhaps his key concept – 'negotiating the curriculum'; in its textual form, itself a major curriculum document of the late 1970s, and subsequently re-published a number of times. The chapter also considers the specific instance of the English curriculum in this regard, and suggests that, while realising the notion in English teaching is quite complicated, it remains nonetheless a powerful and inspiring shaping principle. Chapter 3 focuses on teachers and teaching, and on pedagogy, and is organised by the concept-metaphor of 'teacher power'. It takes up the theme of teachers' relative powerfulness over the past 40-plus years, set against a commitment to professional autonomy and agency, and indicates Boomer's own constant commitment to the profession, and to teaching as a vocation. Chapter 4 addresses more squarely subject English itself. While it notes a certain ambivalence in the curriculum theorising associated with the subject post-Dartmouth, it explores what are undoubtedly some of its key and enduring features, referring particularly to 'literature' and 'writing'. Boomer's views on these and other matters are presented, but also his willingness to take the subject-area into new areas of cultural practice and learning. A final chapter traces the nature and movement of Boomer's later work in what had become increasingly difficult times. By this he had moved far from English teaching *per se* and was operating at senior levels in the educational bureaucracy. He remained interested and committed to the post-Dartmouth project of English teaching, however, seeing it as a resource that continued to enrich his thinking, in navigating the larger scene of Australian education.

Notes

1 Or rather, *mis*-quoting her – Durst rather awkwardly uses the term "scholar/practicioner" (p. 386). Tirrell's somewhat acidic summary account of the North American scene is worth quoting in full: "[B]riefly, the scholar/practitioner walks two traditional roles which until recently have been viewed as quite separate. Scholars are the field's researchers, its philosophers, its knowledge-makers. Practitioners apply the research and knowledge, creating in their different, but also respectable, body of knowledge which Stephen North refers to as 'lore'. Scholars often view themselves as knowledge-makers who pass theoretical insights on (or, sometimes more accurately, down) to practitioners. Theorizing in this sense is a one-way street. The lessons and insights of practice rarely return to inform theory" (Tirrell, 1990, p. 167). Hopefully things have well and truly changed since then.
2 An Australian colloquialism, to be further discussed in the Conclusion – in brief: "a person with apparent disregard for convention; a maverick".
3 Subsequently, as Douglas Barnes argued, it was to be rendered as *action*.
4 The latter including Raymond Williams, and also Gramsci – Bakhtin is also significant in this regard (e.g., Crowley, 2018). The key point here is the notion of language as *practice*.
5 Although rarely referred to, curiously enough, Dewey's influence is clearly apparent here.
6 A relatively new phenomenon in itself, in the UK (Medway et al., 2014) and also in Australia.
7 It was subsequently re-published in 1982 as a chapter in the first *Negotiating the Curriculum* book (Boomer, 1982b) and again, essentially unchanged, in 1992. Subsequent references in this book will be to the 1992 version, unless circumstances decree otherwise.
8 But note that the sentence goes on to describe teaching as "[reduced] to an ancillary of learning", continuing as follows: "And from this perspective we can make our teaching as efficient as may be without taking responsibility off the shoulders of the learner" (Britton, 1973, pp. 15–16) – overall, a symptomatic formulation, I suggest, and directly evocative of what is presented here as the pedagogical paradox.
9 It is worth noting, in retrospect, a comment made by Claire Woods (1985), an Australian English educator with close professional ties to Boomer, in her response to his early essay on the links between computing and writing: "We have no word in English for the notion of a close dialectical relationship between teaching-learning, or learning-teaching" (p. 187). Is this 'didaktik'? – or perhaps 'pedagogy'?
10 Originally presented as a keynote in 1982 at the International Reading Association Convention, Chicago.
11 Boomer described this in 1973 as "a centralised system established along bureaucratic lines", further observing that "the essential military structure still prevails" (Boomer, 1973, p. 64) – a point he reiterated much later (Boomer, 1999a).
12 "After all, what is negotiating the curriculum but a process of mutual compromise between teacher and learner, an agreement to work together on certain tasks in certain ways?" (Boomer, 1988a, p. 231).

2 Negotiating the (English) Curriculum

A signature concept in Garth Boomer's work is the notion of 'negotiating the curriculum'. This is widely recognised as perhaps his most iconic idea, the formulation with which he is indelibly associated: *curriculum-as-negotiation*, as it might be called – a distinctive orientation in curriculum and teaching. It is addressed most directly in two books published a decade apart, one in Australia (Boomer, 1982b) and the other in the USA (Boomer et al., 1992). There are also various commentaries and associated accounts over the past 40 years that can be added to the record, developing both theory and practice. The kernel of the idea developed over the late 1970s, in the specific context of language-and-learning, connecting to projects in a range of subject-areas and levels of schooling. For Boomer, of course, an important focus was always on English teaching and English classrooms, catching the wave of what has been described as more generally a curriculum 'break-out' across Australia, and new manifestations of what he was later to call 'teacher power'. English teachers and educators were deeply involved in the movement, attracted not only by its programmatic emphasis on learners and learning but also by its commitment to social justice. This was entirely consistent with the social turn in English teaching more generally, referenced back to the 1975 IFTE conference, held in York (Dixon, 1975), and with extensive 'progressive' curriculum reform in post-1960s Australia (Yates et al., 2011).

In what follows, I firstly introduce the concept itself, along with a sense of its history in Australia, and beyond. My aim is to focus not so much on what might be called the 'technology' of curriculum negotiation, or its techniques as such, its ways and means, but on the formulation more generally: on Boomer's *conceptualisation* of (a) negotiated curriculum, and hence its organising and shaping principles. The focus turns then to 'programming', or teachers' curriculum design and development work, which was taken up in Australia as an especially important aspect of new thinking in curriculum and schooling, particularly in subject English. I then consider the concept's wider implication, with discussion of 'student voice' and 'democracy', as central issues arising from the negotiation project. Finally, specific implications for subject English are explored, as I address the question of how that project is realised in the field and what it means for rethinking English teaching. It is worth observing at this point, however, that the idea of 'negotiation' has had continuing resonance for Australian English teaching and curriculum

DOI: 10.4324/9781003374886-2

inquiry. In a recent keynote address to the AATE's annual conference, a leading English educator noted: "Negotiation was Boomer's signature theme – the centre of gravity for so much of his work. At its core, negotiation is the expression of democratic values and ethical intentions in teaching and learning, curriculum and power relations" (Manuel, 2023, p. 11). These words provide an excellent stepping-off point for the account to come.

Conceptualising 'Negotiating the Curriculum'

The single most direct statement of what constitutes 'negotiating the curriculum' is as follows:

> Negotiating the curriculum means deliberately planning to invite students to contribute to, and to modify, the educational programme, so that they will have a real investment both in the learning journey and in the outcomes. Negotiating also means making explicit, and then confronting, the constraints of the learning context, and the non-negotiable requirements that apply.
> (Boomer, 1992a, p. 14)

This is described elsewhere as "a theory of teaching and learning" (Boomer et al., 1992, p. ix), although it is perhaps better viewed as marking out an educational philosophy. Elaborating on this, negotiating the curriculum is later described thus: "We know that it is more than a method or technique, that it is a theory of teaching, learning and curriculum composing" (Boomer et al., 1992, p. 195). This is indeed what it became – a distinctive curriculum theory: curriculum-as-negotiation – although this only emerged over considerable time, and through repeated scrutiny and testing. Boomer himself never developed it to this point, understandably, although he certainly pointed out the way. There seems little doubt, however, that he would have been open to such elaborations, given his own interest in curriculum inquiry, preferably practice-referenced and always inclusive of teachers and teaching.[1] The case for 'negotiation' as a distinctive curriculum orientation – set alongside 'transmission' and 'interpretation' – is made much later (Green, 2018b[2]; see also Green, 2021a), and is still to be fully articulated. Nonetheless the importance of the concept, and its continuing resonance, is widely acknowledged.

As already noted, the concept was presented first in 1978, as a paper published somewhat like a manifesto, having been developed as a position paper for a national working-party on the role of language in learning (Boomer, 1978). It was then published again, more formally, as the lead chapter in a book which Boomer edited (Boomer, 1982b). Hence that paper presumably distilled and sought to express succinctly the deliberations of the group involved, and their respective networks across the country. That is important to note.[3] Boomer worked with a range of people, across Australia, as always. The original formulation was therefore part of a more general curriculum movement in Australia at that time, an opening up of possibilities. It linked up with a general process of "grassroots curriculum reform", within which notions of 'negotiation' and accounting more for student involvement figured significantly (Teese, 2014, p. 154).[4] "The curriculum, as a set of demands on students, could not be preconceived and planned without regard to the characteristics and views of students" (Teese, 2014, p. 154). Boomer was looking at the time for a way to bring various (then) emergent reform initiatives together in and for classroom practice, with the notion of 'negotiating the curriculum' emerging as "a strong conception of learning and teaching which required a co-curriculum planning relationship between teachers and students" (Boomer, 1988a, p. 231).

It was, in fact, much more than simply a matter of '(co-)planning', or a form of conjoint 'programming':

> Within such an emergent framework of understanding, ... the project of 'negotiating the curriculum' was always more than simply a pedagogical strategy but, rather – at least potentially – an important socio-political initiative, opening up the possibility of a more critical-dialogical view of curriculum and schooling, and indeed of education and democracy.
>
> (Green, 2018b, p. 87)

That is, the opportunity was thus provided not only to enhance student learning but also to connect this to democratic social practice more generally. But this could not at all be guaranteed, and indeed the struggle that it implied and ushered in quickly became apparent, certainly to Boomer himself. Hence it is important to read beyond the 'Negotiating the Curriculum' paper, to take in both the various case-study accounts and reports that figure in the two main books (Boomer, 1982b; Boomer et al., 1992) and also Boomer's own commentaries and reflections, across a range of papers, if one is to better appreciate the project.[5]

However, the organising idea of 'inviting' students in, as above, is itself clearly important in this regard, and even fundamental. "Negotiation... means deliberately planning the curriculum with the complicity of the students" (Boomer, 1982d, p. 4). It is therefore a way of encouraging students to become involved, indeed invested, and to thereby draw them in, to engage them, which on one level might be seen as above all else pedagogically useful. But it is also much more than this, at least potentially, in that it provides for the possibility of establishing a more active, authentic exchange, a dialogue, a 'partnership' between teacher and learner. This 'invitation' evokes a liberal-humanist view of the classroom, and of education more generally, and perhaps a rather optimistic and even altruistic stance overall. It doesn't allow for the more radical view that became clearer and more insistent in Boomer's work over time, as the following suggests:

> The negotiating teacher ... is at pains to lay bare the workings of the curriculum, to declare, and indeed to co-construct teaching intentions, strategies, and evaluative criteria, at the same time inviting students, within bounds, to contribute to and influence the course of study, its products, and its territorial coverage.
>
> (Boomer, 1993, p. 7)

Yet notions of exchange, invitation, dialogue, etc., are certainly part of the discursive field here, as evident in Britton's (1982, p. 4) insistence on "an interactive view of learning" and language and learning more generally as it is, albeit somewhat differently inflected, in certain Bakhtinian perspectives, if not in Bakhtin himself. 'Negotiation' itself is open to various interpretations, and indeed it might appropriately be described as classically 'multi-accentual'.

These are metaphors, and indeed metaphors figure heavily in Boomer's work, as central to his rhetoric and his pedagogy. They point, in this instance, to the striving that I think can be discerned in his work overall for an adequate language – something akin, perhaps, to Ted Aoki's phenomenology (a perhaps surprising link, picked up in Chapter 3) – which does justice to the experience and the phenomenon he is concerned with, but which may not be available in the pragmatic and even prosaic Australian discursive context. But precisely because they are metaphors, they need to be seen rather warily. In what ways is a teacher-student 'partnership' possible in institutionalised education? This in fact has been noted in various more sceptical and even critical commentaries on the significance of Dartmouth and the new emphasis on language and learning (e.g., Harris, 2012). Then again this was how Boomer worked, characteristically and even programmatically, rhetorically, using metaphors prolifically and sometimes profligately to create a tapestry of sense *and* meaning, leading others into new ways of thinking and acting. Understanding the concept of curriculum negotiation requires, then, engaging with ideas as images and texts, as much as anything else, and this must be taken into account in following through its implications and challenges. The *language* itself is important.

'Negotiation' – Keywords and Other Concepts

It is useful to keep working from the original 'manifesto' paper to provide further insight into the idea of negotiating the curriculum. That paper presented terms which remain pertinent and resonant across the whole trajectory of Boomer's work in this regard. It begins with an assertion of 'learning theory' – and importantly, this is not to be understood in a formal disciplinary ('psychological') sense, but rather with respect to learners themselves, students *and* teachers. The question asked is: How do we learn? How does anyone learn? Learning is understood as making sense of things, in one's own terms and for oneself, working on available information and transforming it in personal 'internally persuasive' understanding. "By learning theory I do not mean being able to précis Piaget, Skinner, and Bruner. I mean being able to state one's own best-educated understandings as to how people come to internalise new information or to perform new operations", Boomer (1992a, p. 5) wrote. Significantly, learning is linked explicitly here with 'theorising'. It is important to see this moreover in terms of *both* students and teachers, *as* learners. Indeed, to focus thus on learning is to bring together *student* learning and *teacher* learning, as shared and even interwoven concerns. Moreover, a strategic shift has occurred here, from focusing on language to focusing on *learning*, in furthering the language-and-learning project.[6]

This leads to a further key point: firstly, the significance of 'theory', and secondly, and relatedly, the idea of 'sharing the theory'. The former is explicitly picked up elsewhere (Boomer, 1988d), where it is presented as a matter of sharing "secrets" – the latter an important notion in itself. But it also refers to theory as 'power', and to sharing power, along with sharing theory. In practical terms, this means, as a teacher, talking about why one is doing this particular activity, and in this way, with the onus always being on teachers to articulate and make clear the reasons for their actions in the classrooms, in their exchanges with students – being 'honest' and 'explicit, and 'coming clean'. Traditionally the balance of power in classroom has been with teachers, whereas now it is conceived as more reciprocating, more of an ebb and flow.[7] Moreover, learning theory cannot be dissociated from a broader curriculum purview:

> learning theory cannot be disconnected from the criteria used to select what is to be learnt and when (i.e., our theory of the *curriculum content*: the subject offerings and the subject sequencing). These, in turn, are framed by a theory about society or culture.
> (Boomer, 1992e, p. 5)

The British educational sociologist Basil Bernstein is evoked in this context, in particular his work on "the framing and sequencing of curriculum" (p. 5), and on the relationship between knowledge and control, and indeed Bernstein constitutes an important influence overall. As Boomer (1992e, p. 5) wrote: "When I think back on many years of work in schools, I think that education is an almost self-perpetuating chain of subjections".

A further crucial keyword therefore is *power*. This remains a constant organising principle, although it is also something which evolves and transmutes across the work. Early on, and indeed from the outset, power is both structural and yet also somewhat metaphorical, as Boomer works through his understandings of the concept in large part through his practice and his experience, thereby enacting his own emerging theory in this regard. Along with Bernstein, as already noted, figures such as Michael Apple and Henry Giroux are increasingly referenced, from the critical education studies context, as is Freire. Later, Boomer engages explicitly with Foucault and, in particular, increasingly works with the notion of power as *productive*, which is linked in turn to agency, notably teachers' agency – something picked up here in Chapter 3.

A definite evolution can be observed in Boomer's understanding of power, then.[8] From what might be described as a left-liberal view, it became more overtly and explicitly socially-critical. Seemingly focused initially on the classroom, it opens up to take on a wider, more social perspective. This is registered in a criticism presented in the 1992 book, with Boomer's original notion of curriculum negotiation, as 'curriculum composing', described as "exclud[ing] the sociopolitical world from its attention and intentions" (Onore & Lubetsky, 1992, p. 255). Boomer explicitly responded to this later in the book, noting the importance of "developing a wider view" of what curriculum negotiation involved, and asserting that "[r]eading the system means going beyond education, especially to a reading of national and international politics and economics" (Boomer, 1992b, p. 283). Elsewhere and much earlier he had written of the need for "reading the whole curriculum", and of the value of developing students' capacity to 'read' school culture, with and against the grain (Boomer, 1988d, p. 155). This suggests the need to turn one's attention explicitly to context, as much as to text (if indeed not more) in developing curriculum. Teachers need, in addition to their own expertise, "a grasp of the political, ideological and material forces that bear upon what happens in the classroom" (Boomer & Torr, 1987, p. 9).

This was especially important to ensure that those not attuned to the dominant culture of curriculum and schooling were involved in the dialogue. That certainly included disadvantaged groups – but it also referred to students more generally in relation to teachers. Teachers not only have the school knowledge, the subject matter, which students want and need, they also have the knowledge of schooling, which includes what counts (i.e., testing and assessment, at the very least).[9] Furthermore, sometimes this can seem obscure, almost wilfully so, and even secretive. The 'secrets' in question are those unspoken things in schooling, or those simply left tacit, whether deliberately or inadvertently, as part of the taken-for-granted. Yet students have differential access to this covert curriculum, depending on their social histories and experiences. Schooling can seem almost 'magical' in this sense, for some. As Boomer (1988d, p. 162) wrote: "What we should be doing, I believe, is saying, 'Come behind here and I'll show you how it [i.e., school] works'. By that I mean, letting students into one's seemingly magic curriculum tricks, or, to put it another way, leaving uncovered the footprints so often carefully dusted over". This means interrupting the magic, or the seemingly obvious, the taken-for-granted. It is that very taken-for-grantedness that he wanted to unsettle, and to challenge. This challenge was firstly directed to teachers, but beyond that, the argument pertains to the middle-class nature of curriculum and schooling, thereby also drawing in those students with congruent cultural capital.

With regard to negotiating the curriculum, undoubtedly Boomer was responding to the traditional situation in classrooms and schools where teachers clearly exercise positional power (as do school leaders), although he was also quick to complicate such a view.[10] His aim was to open up the classroom to a more equitable, indeed more democratic field of relations and exchanges. This is consistent with the increasingly more explicit social and political perspective emerging in English teaching at that time, often identified with the 1975 York IFTE conference in the UK, an important successor-event to Dartmouth. It was certainly evident elsewhere as well, including in Australia, and in the critical pedagogy movement. Importantly, power is increasingly conceived as something *exercised*, and on various levels, including that of the classroom. Power is not outside and above, bearing down, rather it is realised in and through *practices*, including the textual and material practices of teaching and learning. (Chapter 3 indicates Boomer's growing awareness of practice theory and philosophy – to which might be added a further point about the significance here of Pragmatist philosophy.)

In this context it is appropriate to point to another key term mobilised here: *demystification*. This links up with constant injunctions to be explicit, and to 'come clean', as already noted. Explicitness is evoked because of Boomer's recognition that much of school culture tends to be tacit, something one learns, or acquires, in the course of living in and through it. But it is also differentially obscure, depending on one's history and experience, one's social trajectory. For some it can be unfamiliar, at the very least, and even strange, unsettling, or indeed alien and threatening. What does one do in such circumstances, Boomer asks? The more alien it seems, the more estranged one feels, the less one is inclined to take a risk, to respond to a teacher's questions, or open up to their invitations. Instead, as the expression goes, these are the students who tend to pull their heads in, who keep silent (or are they silenced?), managing as best they can, or else effectively opting out. The notion of 'demystification', although clearly related, does different work here, pushing out from simply being 'explicit' about teachers' reasons for doing what they do in the classroom – even to themselves, sometimes. It serves to encompass the effects of power, working at different levels but also realised through practice, in its everyday normative character, and also in more recognisable ways (in high-stakes final examinations, for instance). "There will always be inequalities of power in both schools and society", Boomer (1992a, p. 8) asserted, "and the effects of power will be offset only if those in power make quite explicit the values, assumptions and criteria on which they base their action". As he went on to say: "In this way others will have a better chance to defend themselves, more opportunity to question and more chance of negotiation, at least where the power figure is not entirely despotic" (p. 8).

This raises many questions, of course: he is implicitly referring to ideology here, and it can be asked how much is ideology accessible to consciousness and rationality? Boomer's focus on "values, assumptions and criteria" is understandable, though, given what he is endeavouring to achieve pedagogically (and bureaucratically). The point is, he was very much aware of power, in all its forms of expression – including the ideological. His call for 'demystification' was undoubtedly part of this, as was his constant emphasis on reflexivity, even though clearly there are limits in this regard. These are important issues of ideology, discourse, and subjectivity, which others have engaged with explicitly, and they come out in his reference elsewhere to Brechtian motifs and strategies, and to what might be called a pedagogy of estrangement (see Chapter 3). While it is true that foregrounding 'demystification' had a certain romanticism about it, early on, it also indicates his awareness of power, and the social dynamics of reproduction and resistance, which later modulates into what he comes to call a "pragmatic-radical" stance, more appropriate for working within systems and regimes.

Hence a further keyword from the very outset, and extremely important, is that of *constraints*. This speaks to Boomer's constant emphasis not only on what works – an eminently pragmatic orientation, albeit always informed by principle – but also on what is possible, in prevailing circumstances. What is it that constrains teaching for learning? What acts upon teaching and learning to limit opportunities for their best expression? This was later identified with the common formulation

'Yes, but...'. "Between the advocacy and the action... falls a curtain", Boomer (1988e, p. 195) wrote, "It is a curtain of questions and doubts, a veil of 'yes, buts'". This means always taking context into consideration – reckoning contexts into account, as necessary and unavoidable, both locally and globally. "Teachers are continually at war with *contexts*, trying to make them hospitable to their intentions" (Boomer, 1988e, p. 196); "teaching is a constrained and contested act" (p. 196). Constraints are therefore central to curriculum negotiation. One is constantly working with and against contexts and their affordances, negotiating constraints as much as subject matter or student learning outcomes. "Eventually, no matter how brilliant and resourceful the teacher, the classroom action will always represent some kind of uneasy armistice between personal knowledge and intentions on the one hand and contextual and interpersonal demands on the other" (Boomer, 1988e, p. 196). Pragmatically radical, he argued that constraints are to be seen along what is described as 'non-negotiables' – due consideration, and acceptance, of those things that simply must be lived with, and worked through: jurisdictional and curricular mandates, for instance, something which becomes increasingly evident as time passes and history unfolds.

This emphasis on power, on constraints and limits, is crucial to curriculum negotiation, then: working with and against the grain of the educational system as a whole. It is not, moreover, that such matters are *essentially* non-negotiable, or that they aren't open to criticism and contestation, and to be struggled over. It is, rather, that it is best to do so when and as the opportunity arises, and it becomes possible – or more likely – to have some effect. It is about working strategically *and* tactically: the hallmark, in fact, of what Boomer was later to call the 'pragmatic-radical' teacher.[11]

'Programming' – Teachers' Curriculum Work

A key practical issue is that of *programming*[12] – that is, teachers' 'planning', as classroom-level curriculum design and development work. This became a major concern of curriculum and teaching in the post-60s era, certainly in Australia, with teachers charged with preparing units of work for their classes, often in the absence of elaborated curriculum guidelines. It was, moreover, even more relevant in English teaching, given the movement towards relatively brief and succinct syllabus statements and associated guidelines. Teachers were increasingly seen as responsible, as individual practitioners, for generating detailed curriculum statements, outlining focus, scope, sequence, continuity, and development, and bringing together content and method, as well as assessment. Boomer was particularly interested in this issue, as a marker of both professional agency and the effective shaping of classroom curriculum, or 'quality' teaching and learning (cf. Reid, 2013, p. 40). Programming can be seen, in fact, as central to the theory and practice of curriculum negotiation. This is somewhat paradoxical, given that programming is commonly seen as something done prior to classroom practice, and as its prospective representation – as a particular form of (regulated) 'writing', or written preparation. But that needs to be understood appropriately, and programming itself reconceptualised (e.g., Green, 1990a; Reid, 2013). Boomer provides an innovative and complex view of programming, as it happens, and in explicit relation to curriculum negotiation. Picking up on the notion of a pedagogy of the *question*, he suggests that, firstly, quality questions matter; secondly, it is learners who need to be asking them; and thirdly, genuine questions encourage engagement. Asking the question connects with the power of intention.[13] This pedagogy of the question, moreover, is to be realised at every level, in the relationship between unit-planning and lesson-planning, and within and across curriculum units, or mini-courses of study.

A crucial consideration, then, is the set of key questions seen as organising curriculum and teaching, precisely as curriculum negotiation. Boomer (1992c, p. 39) presents them thus, expressly from the point of view of the student/Other:

- What do we already know?
- What do we need to know?

Note that these questions are to be understood as *posed by the students*, the prospective learners, first of all, and secondly, that they are addressed to the class, the community of inquiry ('us', 'we'), working together. In more elaborated form:

- What do we know already? (or: Where are we now, and what don't we need to find out or be taught about?)
- What do we want, and need, to find out? (or: What are our questions, what don't we know, and what are our problems, curiosities and challenges?)
- How will we go about finding out? (or: Where will we look, what experiments and inquiries will we make, what will we need, what information and resources are available, who will do what, and what should be the order of things?)
- How will we know, and show, that we've found when we're finished? (or: What are our findings, what have we learnt, whom will we show and for whom are we doing the work, and where next?) (Cook, 1992, p. 21)

Boomer (1992c, pp. 39–44) provides, in turn, a somewhat elaborated and more focused version of these questions, filtered through his own account of programming. "Whether planning this year's program or a specific unit of work over, say, two weeks", he writes, this involves due consideration of "the following seven element of curriculum planning" (p. 35): content / justification of content / products / skills and media / learning activities / aids and resources / methods of evaluation.[14] Boomer's own exposition of the movement from initial thinking, planning and imagining to later realisations of the unit in thought and in action, through to reflection upon it and evaluation, remains instructive. What is distinctive about this account is, firstly, the manner in which it moves across and between speech and writing, practice and representation; and secondly, its deliberate deployment of the metaphor of "curriculum composing". Hence it has been described as effectively a 'Reconceptualist' account (Green, 1990a, 2018c), even though that was certainly not how it was originally presented or understood. That is, programming is to be perceived not so much as 'planning' as 'composing' activity – a shift, that is, from 'planning' to 'composing', as an organising principle. This means that, rather than being seen as pro-scriptive and more or less a matter of prior cognition, it is a form of textual practice intricately connected with, and interwoven into, curriculum practice. As described elsewhere: "Programming is… best conceived, and practised, as a composing activity, and this involves seeing it emphatically in terms of thinking and meaning" (Green, 1990a, pp. 48–49) – but also as 'imagining'.

> Garth Boomer has continually stressed the importance of 'imagining' in curriculum and learning, and this can be specifically linked to the view of *programming as a way of conceptualizing the classroom as vividly as possible, projecting oneself into the future in such a way as to indwell in it.*
>
> (Green, 1990a, p. 48 – emphasis added here)

Boomer's constant emphasis on 'story' is pertinent here, too, and indeed curriculum as *story*.[15] In this regard, it is notable that he presents the negotiating-the-curriculum process in terms of an epic narrative, a quest or journey, comprising 'The Challenge', 'The Preparation', 'The Search', 'The Test', and 'The Reflection' (Boomer, 1992c, p. 34), with learners cast as protagonists, 'heroes', agential figures seeking the prize of meaning. The significance of this lies in the way that pleasure, affect and desire figure in curriculum and schooling; these key human drives do not always emerge in more technocratic and cognitivist, linear-rationalist perspectives, too often characteristic of mainstream research and policy.

Returning to Boomer's superordinate questions: To foreground asking, at the outset, *What do we know already?* flies in the face of the grammar of schooling (Tyack & Tobin, 1994; see also Tyack & Cuban, 1995), and in particular, the logic of the recitation (Blacker, 2017). This presupposes that it is teachers who initiate curriculum activity, asking the opening question, which is followed by the learner's response, and – a third move – is then evaluated, *by the teacher* once again. This is effectively the traditional IRE (Initiation-Response-Evaluation) sequence, which can be seen as the normative discourse structure of schooling. Not only do teaching and the teacher occupy two out of the three available speaking-positions, but these constitute effectively a *frame* – so that learning is thereby always-already framed by teaching. This is entirely contrary to the arguments and assertions of language-and-learning theory, as previously noted. Britton (1970, 1982) and Barnes (1976), among others (Wells, 1995, 1999), provide the basis for positing a counterview, one which shifts the focus to *learning*, first off, and then, *teaching-learning*. Indeed, Boomer's whole position is congruent with Britton's (1982) important stress on "[a]dult *and* child-centred" education, as "interactive learning", and his "highlighting [of] the crucial role of language, in its many modes, as the principal instrument of interaction" (Britton, 1982, pp. 3–4; my added emphasis).

What do we know already? – this is above all else to draw students in, to ask what it is they already know about this particular topic, this subject matter. They are thus invited in, and encouraged to lay out their existing knowledge, to make it explicit and visible, and to articulate it, and in some cases, to validate it, perhaps. Teachers need to know this, in turn: "A good deal of wasteful teaching occurs where teachers do not rigorously check what the children already know before they begin a new unit" (Boomer, 1988e, p. 200). This is the case today, surely, with mandated curriculum and related forms of prescription and regulation increasingly the norm. What is the first question teachers ask, in beginning a new unit of work, first in selecting what it is to be, and secondly, in that initial encounter with the class, in the classroom? Boomer would have us attend to *both* these moments or phases, in each instance actively imagining and inviting the learners into a shared enterprise, a common, collaborative undertaking, a rich *curriculum* experience. It is this sense that "curriculum composing", as he understands it, and "programming for learning" come together in the practice and project of negotiating the curriculum. How are *this* subject matter and *these* students to be brought together? That depends, in part, on their congruency, although the quality and pertinence of *what is being studied* is also clearly important: "A unit of work without solid *content* will be 'at risk'" (Boomer, 1992c, p. 36). Yet Boomer is also emphasising the priority of the teacher–student relationship, *for the teacher*, who must therefore put his or her concern for knowledge or the discipline, the 'content', into abeyance – at least temporarily, or provisionally. This is neither to deny nor to diminish it, rather it is to acknowledge the complexity of pedagogy, as Boomer sees and enacts it.

Teachers matter in this context. It is the teacher who sets the scene and establishes the parameters, and s/he cannot, and should not, abdicate this professional responsibility. But then s/he enters into negotiation *at each and every point* with the students, who learn through experience how to engage in curriculum dialogue of this kind. Boomer (1992d, p. 33) has provided, informally, a succinct summary-account of curriculum negotiation:

> first of all the teacher goes away and draws up a script which is the imagining of how the story will go, the teacher then brings the script to class and the teacher has more or less negotiation with [the class]; the moment it's brought into the classroom and you get into enactment the script starts to change and the story starts to change and at various points then between the presentation of the course and the development of the product, the completion of the assignment, at various point on my model ... you could at any time stop and evaluate it and do a replay, say 'OK, how did that bit go?', 'What do you think will happen next?'.

Curriculum, as he formulates it, "is a process beginning with the teacher's or the curriculum writer's conception, proceeding through planning, and eventually reaching enactment and evaluation" (Boomer, 1992c, p. 33). Students are drawn in – ideally they enter willingly into what is in effect a 'contract', a mutual agreement – and thereby become co-producers of the curriculum story. Not that this ever happens all at once, or without practice and commitment, and appropriate conditions, and nor does it happen uniformly, in each and every classroom. Boomer was very clear about this, right from the outset: "Fully fledged negotiation is rarely possible in the beginning" (Boomer, 1982d, p. 5). This is why the focus needs to be placed, firmly and clearly, on curriculum negotiation as principle, as theory, as philosophy. Programming, properly understood as "a creative, intellectual act" (Howie, 2006, p. 234) on the part of teachers as engaged professionals, is a central aspect.

On 'Student Voice' and 'Democracy'

Two key points need to be explored here. One is the notion of 'student voice' – another metaphor – and the other is that of democracy. Indeed the two are best considered together, in furthering our understanding of the project of negotiating the curriculum. Exploring this has been undertaken by various commentators (e.g., Bron et al., 2022; Cook-Sather, 2006; Mayes, 2013), and what follows builds on such discussion. Taking due account of 'student voice' is clearly crucial to curriculum-as-negotiation. This is indicated in central formulations such as "invit[ing] students to contribute to, and to modify, the educational programme" and stressing "student readiness to ask questions – procedural, substantive and speculative" (Boomer, 1992c, p. 288). The result is to open up curriculum development *and* classroom practice to the perspective of the Other – in this instance, the student, the learner. This is, above all, an issue of *agency*. For Mayes (2013, p. 62), there are important convergences "between the concepts of 'negotiating the curriculum' and 'student voice'", with 'student voice' presented as "a pedagogical movement that seeks to shift the 'locus of authority'... in schools". This view is strongly endorsed further and more fully illuminated in Cook-Sather's (2006) account of the 'student voice' movement, traced across Australia, Canada, England, and the United States, in which she associates the notion of "[h]aving a voice" with "having presence, power, and agency" (p. 363). At the very least, the effect is to bring students forward and up-front, to foreground them and involve them more in educational decision-making and debate, and to take them more actively and explicitly into account, as capable and responsible actors – as *agents*.

Asking questions such as 'What do we/you know already?' and 'What do we/you want and need to know?' accordingly opens the door. It also puts the emphasis on the relationship itself (*we/you*). What kind of relationship is this? What are we (*I/you*) here for? What brings us together? What is the significance of the outcome? On what level(s)? Student learning is certainly important in this regard, and indeed crucial – if it hasn't occurred, for whatever reason, can this be seen as anything other than a failed or flawed pedagogy? But arguably there is also a larger social practice happening in and alongside this, which can be understood as a matter of social (re)production. It is at this point that it becomes necessary to shift attention to the question of democracy.

Much has been made of the implications of curriculum negotiation for democracy, in the classroom and, beyond that, the school, and perhaps more widely still. Much has also been written about education and democracy (e.g., Apple & Beane,

2007; Riddle & Apple, 2019), and more specifically education *for* democracy. This has been directly linked to curriculum negotiation, with the emphasis firmly placed on the *practice* of democracy. As Bron et al. (2022, p. 47) write:

> [T]he participation of students in curriculum negotiation is an example of practi[s]ing democratic principles. Through their participation, students practice democratic skills that are also the focal point of citizenship education. By negotiating with peers and teachers, students practise and practise cooperation, communication and decision-making.

At its simplest, this means involving students more actively in their own education, as co-makers of curriculum. This is appropriately understood however as having a stake in their future, given that education is always not simply an investment in the future but also its production, calling it into being. Hence it is entirely reasonable that students should have a say in it, an agentive, participatory, co-productive role. This may be all the more imperative in the present time, marked as it is by the urgencies and emergencies of climate change. As Brennan et al. (2022) note: "Students… continue to be the object of curricular reform, stifling their voices and participation, as well as that of parents, community members and teachers, to influence the purposes and entrenched practices of curriculum activity" (p. 320). This is notwithstanding the current rise of student climate activism, worldwide. While Boomer was working more in the context of the post-1960s generational turmoil, there are similarities in the emergence on the scene of new voices and energies, breaking through the surface and challenging business as usual. He was definitely responding to the traditional view of students as simply 'objects' of educational practice. This was alongside and linked to the New English's recognition of learning and difference as distinctive features of (then) contemporary schooling (e.g., Burgess, 1988). What Boomer drew in, however, was a new sensitivity to students ('student power') as the emergent constituency of schools, as the citizens of the future. This is at the heart of curriculum-as-negotiation, moreover, with students thereby recognised as 'subjects', and agents of history.

Moreover, it is worth considering here how democracy itself is understood. In recent work, reference is commonly made to two forms: 'deliberative democracy', emphasising reason and argument, and a more radical position focused on what is called 'agonistic democracy', which allows more for conflict and unassimilable difference (e.g., Green, 2018c, Chapter 2). Boomer allows for both of these, in highlighting language and negotiation. Coming to agreement, a shared view, is clearly part of the process, and it is likely that this will characterise much of what happens in classroom settings. However, what about those where there are marked (social) differences to contend with, with little opportunity for easy or ready resolution. In such instances, it is more the case that the parties involved – teacher and student(s) – simply come to some sort of settlement, allowing things to go on. In some instances they won't, and that is always also a possibility. Nonetheless: "The negotiating teacher is committed to changing the balance of power in the classroom and to establishing a climate and relationship in which student dissent, difference, and preference is heard and to some extent accommodated and mobilized" (Boomer, 1993, p. 7).

Something worth observing at this point is how challenging it has become to consider 'negotiating the curriculum' in 21st century Australia, in the context of a legislated national curriculum. What is there to be negotiated, when so much of formal curriculum and assessment is now mandated? What room is there to move? Boomer would argue that there are always opportunities and possibilities in curriculum policy and even in its seemingly most closed texts. Besides, there is clearly space for interpretation on the part of teachers, schools, and systems in the Australian Curriculum – though whether or not this is realised is another matter entirely.[16] Nonetheless it is possible to highlight here certain initiatives which seem relevant and promising. Zipin and colleagues draw on the 'funds of knowledge' literature in proposing that an important focus in current circumstances is what is called "problems that matter". As they write: "We imagine building dynamic curriculum activity around problems that matter (PTMs) in students' lifeworld locales, linked to global crises for social futures, as strong attractors of richly diverse and useful knowledge" (Zipin & Brennan, 2024, p. 41). Importantly this concept is tied to students and student activism, particularly with regard to climate change. Zipin and colleagues express concern about the limits of the Australian Curriculum, observing that "[c]entralised control of curriculum and associated assessment leave very little curricular space or pedagogic time for students to address issues of deep concern to them" (Brennan et al., 2022, p. 320). As noted elsewhere: "Does the curriculum fail the test of meaningful relevance to students' present and future lives?" (Taylor et al., 2020, p. 3).

This notion of 'problems that matter' would seem an excellent opportunity for curriculum negotiation, with students working "in collaboration with teachers, academics, and local-community people" (Zipin & Brennan, 2024, p. 41) to construct a meaningful, praxis-oriented curriculum, thereby co-producing an educational experience at once significant and deeply relevant. Deweyian in its impulse, this is much akin to the best work in post-Dartmouth English teaching organised in terms of 'themes' and the like (also 'rich tasks', etc. – see Tremmel, 2010). Given increasing disaffection and even alienation among school students, and even anxiety, such a perspective might offer real possibilities for re-energising English teaching. It should be noted, finally, that while the current work on 'problems that matter' and the like tends to be focused on 'content', or 'really worthwhile knowledge', there is still a need for teachers' technical skills and professional expertise in shaping the curriculum to best (learning) effect. This is over and beyond their active participation in the curriculum 'story', in the dialogues and exchanges of the classroom and the material meaning-making itself. Hence student participation and democratic practice are brought together in the space of the classroom, spilling out into the local community and beyond.[17]

A number of questions arise at this point. If students are indeed to be viewed as co-curriculum makers, jointly composing the curriculum, what are the limits of such involvement and such activity? That question is crucial to the relationship between curriculum and democracy. This is especially so when curriculum is understood as dynamic and emergent – as something fully realised and appreciated retrospectively, as Boomer (1992c, p. 33) insisted: "Curriculum, in the sense in which I use it, can… be described and fully comprehended only in retrospect", and moreover, in and through practice. The same goes for democracy, which as Derrida insists is better seen as always becoming, and hence as a 'promise', something always and yet 'to come'. Moreover, as he says: "We don't have to wait for future democracy to happen, to appear, we have to do right here and now what has to be done for it" (Derrida, cited in Bennington, 1997). At issue here is democratic *practice*. Accordingly, curriculum is to be understood, as much as anything else, as enacting and realising democracy, both in the here-and-now and historically, in the becoming-future. It matters greatly how things play out in the classroom, then. This was always central to Boomer's vision, and specifically so regarding curriculum-as-negotiation.

The 'Eternal Triangle'

Here it might be helpful to bring in what Boomer (1992a, p. 4) calls "the eternal triangle of education – the *teacher*, the *child* and the *curriculum*". Echoing Dewey and anticipating the introduction into Anglo contexts of *Didaktik* studies, a subsequently important European resource for curriculum inquiry[18] (Green, 2021a; Hopmann, 2007), this formulation is particularly interesting in gauging Boomer's distinctive perspective. A three-way relationship, it indicates how teacher and student (aka the 'child') come together to 'negotiate' what is effectively a third term – 'the curriculum'. What *is* the curriculum? What *counts* as the curriculum? For whom? These are some of the questions that might well arise, pointing to a new emphasis on reflexivity in such matters: a meta-awareness regarding curriculum, not only on the part of teachers but of students as well. Curriculum itself is problematised; it can be (re-)negotiated. There is also a suggestion that teaching-learning thus has strategic priority over subject matter, or curriculum-as-content. But it is that relationship – between teacher and student(s) – that needs to be explored further, to fully grasp what is at issue here. Boomer presents it as, ideally, a partnership, a collaboration, a conjoint activity of curriculum composing.

Something needing to be addressed, then, is the question of the *teacher*'s role and significance in that relationship, and more specifically the teacher's authority and expertise. Boomer always saw curriculum negotiation as something to move towards, to *develop* skills and confidence in, on the part of *both* teachers and students. This is the case for a range of reasons, from the mundane to the more complicated. Getting started and coming to know what is needed and what is at risk involves building the relationship itself, and that takes time and effort, and commitment. This is always on the basis of a fundamental asymmetry, an inequality of powers: "After all, what is negotiating the curriculum but a process of mutual compromise between teacher and learner, an agreement to work together on certain tasks in certain ways?" – moreover, it is always "a negotiation between unequals, in that teachers have the positional power, the experiential power and the power of sanctions (pass or fail)" (Boomer, 1988a, p. 231). This is where the teacher's expertise comes in. S/he knows about curriculum structure: how to construct a curriculum, a course of study, in such a way as to develop student learning, as 'coming to know'. There is undoubtedly a technical element to curriculum and ideally teachers are trained and knowledgeable in how to provide the best environment for its optimal development. This is indeed one source of teachers' authority, as well as being a key marker of their expertise. Students come to recognise and acknowledge that expertise and its associated authority, both in their accumulated experience of schooling and in the relationship they co-construct with their teachers in the here-and-now, and over time. Negotiating the curriculum is one way to enable this to happen, to best effect – and arguably a particularly rich and productive context for doing so.

Hence it is important to see that there is no question here of abdicating the teacher's role and significance: "negotiation is not an abrogation of the mandate to teach" (Boomer, 1993, p. 9). Teaching becomes something different, however, at least from current-traditional 'transmissionary' views.[19] It becomes a matter of tact and timing, strategy and tactics, at once responsive and improvisational, and yet always purposive, and informed by an overall vision, a teleology. This certainly includes bringing together the 'what' and the 'how' and the 'why' in particular curriculum units and episodes but also, arguably, for larger and longer-term educational practices and trajectories. Above all, it is political as well as pedagogic, bringing together student learning and social change.

Addressing the English Curriculum

It remains now to focus more specifically on English teaching in this context, and on the idea of negotiating the *English* curriculum. That is because, right from the very outset, a considerable part of the negotiating-the-curriculum literature deals with a range of subject-areas and even different levels of schooling. This, in turn, is consistent with the post-60s project of language and learning and the language and literacy across the curriculum movement, as a key reference-point here. Even so, an affinity clearly exists between English teaching, especially post-Dartmouth, and the curriculum negotiation initiative. Boomer himself was an English teacher originally, and he remained connected and close to the field throughout his career. What needs to be taken into account here, however, is that increasingly he was working with constituencies other than the English teaching profession, and with teachers and teaching more generally, and this meant in effect becoming more engaged with what we might now call curriculum inquiry.

Indeed his work is also usefully read within that context, and explicitly so. It has been proposed, in fact, that he is to be associated with a third curriculum orientation, with 'negotiation' joining 'transmission' and 'interpretation' as distinctive orientations in curriculum and schooling (Green, 2021a). Curriculum inquiry as such was in its relative infancy at the time Boomer was writing, especially in Australia but also arguably in the UK (Green, 2003b). Yet his work provides a significant contribution in this regard, more particularly at the classroom curriculum level. He observed early on that curriculum was commonly understood as a noun, whereas he saw it as a verb, claiming that "[w]e reified and 'nouned' what can only be a verb" (Boomer, 1984, p. 58), hence the preponderance of references to 'the curriculum', etc. – something that can be seen as persisting today.[20] A new way of thinking was needed. Accordingly, a key statement is as follows: "The curriculum is no longer a prepackaged course to be taken; it is a jointly enacted composition that grows and changes as it proceeds. A new definition is needed, and new ways of evaluating it must be found" (Boomer, 1992c, p. 32). Curriculum is therefore best conceived as an *activity*: "It would be ideologically offensive to coin the term 'curriculuming', but that is what I mean when I think of 'curriculum'". He continues thus, in a passage worth presenting in full:

> Curriculum is a process beginning with the teacher's or the curriculum writer's conception, proceeding through planning, and eventually reaching enactment and evaluation. Ideally, the enterprise is directed towards promoting valued knowledge, abilities and attitudes in the learner, where 'valued' encompasses the world view of both teacher and learner. *Curriculum, in the sense in which I use it, can therefore only be described and fully comprehended only in retrospect.* The quality and scope of what children learn, both foreseen and unforeseen, are the proper focus of evaluation.
>
> (Boomer, 1992c, p. 33; my added emphasis)

While there is much that might be explored in such a formulation, its insight remains powerful, perhaps especially in an age of increasingly mandated curriculum and assessment. Crucially however it is presented explicitly in the context of one of Boomer's most elaborated and distinctive accounts of curriculum negotiation, which he labels as "Curriculum Composing and Evaluating".[21] A central feature of that account, furthermore, is his views on *programming*, or curriculum planning, at the classroom level – which has been described earlier as particularly pertinent to English teaching and indeed to curriculum negotiation.

So when Boomer speaks of 'negotiating *the* curriculum', what is he referring to? Presumably this is in the first instance the *material* curriculum, the espoused or designed curriculum, or what Goodson called the written curriculum – the curriculum as object, or as third term, as 'it'. For much of the school curriculum, this can be readily recognised in the school-subjects, and more particularly in the so-called 'content' areas. Subject English is different in this regard, however; or, at the very least, it provides a challenge to the knowledge question, as it has come to be known in contemporary curriculum debate. Knowledge is arguably of a different order in subject English, being in some ways less framed and organised by the logic of disciplinarity (cf. Green, 2018c, see Chapter 11). In Australia, moreover, while there was less of an emphasis on curriculum as an elaborated syllabus and more emphasis on providing guidelines and directives, in the 1970s, this changed quite soon after, with ongoing and indeed mounting debate, directed especially at subjects like English. All the same it is important to come to an adequate understanding of what constitutes (the) English curriculum, as perceived both retrospectively and synoptically, as the object or focus of negotiation. This means having a sense of 'course' and 'content' – that is, course of study, on the one hand, and subject matter, on the other hand, or the 'what' of teaching-learning.

In the case of English, this commonsensically involves some combination of literature, writing, and language-work, or 'grammar' (see Chapter 4). Teachers and students share a sense of what English looks like, based on their past experience. This is precisely what is up for negotiation, to some extent. Teachers have a developed, disciplinary sense, while students are becoming-disciplined, as it were – although the question of disciplinarity itself is complicated in the case of subject English. Moreover, the subject involves what might be called a *permeable* curriculum, one which is less insulated from the outside, in the form of student experience and funds of knowledge but also popular culture and the media. At the time (i.e., the 1970s), there was also a growing reaction to the fragmentation associated with traditional timetabling practices, with the traditional focus on lesson planning, usually each day across the week, and a shift in emphasis accordingly on larger contexts of meaning-making and units of study of between two and four weeks duration, and a shift to process-developmental programming. What was needed therefore was that students come to understand and appreciate this way of working, something which could only happen through practice and experience. But it also required a certain measure of meta-communication about (the) curriculum, either teacher-initiated or prompted by student questioning. 'This is what we are doing, and this is why we are doing it'. Teacher and students(s) learn over time how to work together, in a sense sharing the theory and co-composing the curriculum.

Another consideration is that subject English was also changing at this time, in accordance with the principles of the New English. A greater emphasis was placed on talk, on talking and writing for learning, on collaboration and small groupwork, on drawing in student and community voices and drawing on student experience, culture, and history. This meant significant changes and challenges in terms of the traditional English curriculum, with literature, for instance, less automatically aligned with the British tradition, and a loosening of the nexus between curriculum and canon. What counted as 'English' was increasingly in question – or, put another way, it was open for negotiation. Cultural authority was increasingly problematised, as was pedagogic authority. The way was thus opened up to heightened forms of exchange, of interaction, between teachers and students, adults and young people, across generations and cultures. The curriculum was not set in stone; it was not monumental, nor in any way natural; rather, it was constructed; it could be questioned and challenged, and it could be changed. As Boomer (1988d, p. 154) wrote: "Curriculum is never 'natural', or inevitable". He frequently referred to figures such as Brecht and Barthes in this regard (something further discussed in Chapter 3 here), describing the curriculum at one point as "a kind of Hollywood western town teaching set" (Boomer, 1988d, p. 162) and observing that "[w]hen you start asking such questions of the school's curriculum, it is no longer possible to think of it as 'natural'" (Boomer, 1988d, p. 157). This is an invitation to view curriculum as *text*, as written, as available for reading *and* (re-)writing.[22] It is one aspect, then, of negotiating the English curriculum.

A further issue is that of making decisions about what texts to study in the English classroom. This is often principally to be seen as a matter of which *literary* texts, although that needs now to be widened to include cinematic and televisual texts, and more recently computer games and other digital arts media. Selection tends still to be within a literary frame, however. Of course, it is never simply about choosing any text at all, from an open field, since there are always constraints of access and availability, as well as those of a budgetary and financial nature. Within this frame, however, there may well be room to move in terms of being pragmatic and working within whatever are the prevailing circumstances. Beyond that, working with a particular text or perhaps a set of texts (an 'intertext') provides opportunity for negotiated reading (Anson, 2021), with the teacher providing access to dominant and disciplinary interpretations and students working from more oppositional and personal perspectives, as well as from their own immediate aesthetic and rhetorical responses. Similarly, writing pedagogy is usefully and appropriately considered in terms of curriculum negotiation, for instance in what was called 'conferencing': the exchange around a draft-text of the student writer and their teacher, with a view to sharpening and developing its articulation of meaning and its effectiveness. The point is that the teacher is open to the exchange, and indeed invites and encourages it, seeing the student(s) as a co-maker of curriculum. This is always in a complex, worldly situation, as a constrained field of curriculum possibility. You start from wherever you are, professionally and more immediately, and always with particular designs: "You have to have some idea of where you are going. ... I don't think you can negotiate everything with kids. There have to be some givens – curriculum givens" (Morgan, 1997, p. 114). Getting there, getting to that point, is what counts. And so is an informed, committed sense of negotiation as an organising principle, a distinctive orientation to curriculum and schooling.

There is one final aspect to consider here, in terms of negotiating the English curriculum. This concerns the figure of the English teacher him- or herself. Boomer was particularly interested in this matter. As he wrote, relatively early on: "Teachers teach most profoundly what they are at the core" (Boomer, 1988g, p. 31). This much-quoted albeit deeply ambivalent statement is discussed further in Chapter 3. He later expressed it more generally thus: "Teaching, at the core, is a demonstration of the self, a generous invitation to students to observe how the teacher thinks, feels, understands, solves, and acts" (Boomer, 1993, p. 10). The implication is, I think, the English teacher is a particular object of scrutiny, in the classroom, but also elsewhere. There is something *symbolic* about English teaching, or rather the *figure* of the English teacher. This is over and beyond their empirical presence. Sawyer (2013, p. 35) describes this in terms of "the teacher/institution-as-text", linking it to a critical literacy perspective. His account suggests that there is a particular sense in which the English *curriculum* is often identified with the English *teacher*, which suggests in turn that the relationship between teacher and student(s) is, in part, what is available to be negotiated. That is an intriguing idea, and certainly it is indeed the case that English teachers historically have been seen as mediating the English curriculum in distinctive ways.

An intriguing link exists in this regard with recent work on the so-called knowledge question in curriculum and schooling, and an argument put forward about the particular significance of 'knower-structures' in school-subjects like English – that is, the priority of 'knowers' (and 'knowing') over 'knowledge'.[23] The case to be made here is that it is the English teacher who most immediately embodies this 'knower-structure', as in effect the subject of English, the emulable subject, the person(age) that the English student most wants to be (or not...). Negotiating the curriculum in English then is, as much as anything else, addressed to how English teachers themselves demonstrate "how to make and take meanings, what to attend to in literature and life, how to make linguistic and life choices, how to be an English teacher and what English is" (Boomer, 1988g, p. 31), *and* how their students make sense of this.

Conclusion: A Bigger Picture?

What are the larger implications and challenges of the negotiating the curriculum project? To answer this involves acknowledging that, while initially and even centrally focused on the classroom, it must be seen as going beyond that, certainly into the school and its community but also beyond that too, into education and society more generally. Boomer explicitly recognises this in extending his argument and advocacy to educational bureaucracies and systems, congruent with his own movement from one position to another and his ongoing reflexive awareness of the associated (and inescapable) complexities and compromises. It is also suggested in observations such as those of John Elliott (1998), who endorsed the notion of educational change as "the negotiated adjustment of society" (p. 61) and the role and significance of teachers in this regard. As Elliot put it: "A 'negotiated' national curriculum would be continuously constructed and reconstructed in an interlocking network of local (school level), regional (local government level) and national forums" (p. 61).[24] This is entirely consistent with Boomer's own view, although his work predated national curriculum initiatives in Australia. As he writes, apropos education and democracy: "the principles underlying the democratic classroom should be congruent with the principles underpinning the [educational] bureaucracy" (Boomer, 1999d, p. 107).

In an open 'letter' to James Britton, Boomer acknowledged the necessity of compromise, as Britton had once advised him, as a strategic principle, and observed that in Australia "[w]e are also coming to understand that, to enable teachers to apply the principles of language and learning, that you have advocated, we need to change the ruling discourse and the containing structures of society" (Boomer, 1988a, p. 240). This means moving beyond the classroom, critical as that is as a social 'microcosm', and Boomer increasing turned his attention in this regard to the larger forums of schools, community, 'systems', and society. It is worth noting here that his 1988 paper was entitled "negotiating the system". (This later phase of Boomer's work is picked up here in Chapter 5.) More generally: "Negotiating the curriculum has become an economic and cultural imperative as, in a fractured and multifarious world, we seek to find the means of sustainable evolution" (Boomer, 1992b, p. 289). It is this kind of vision, then, that warrants proper assessment of curriculum-as-negotiation.

Notes

1 Boomer was an early member of the Australian Curriculum Studies Association and chaired the organising group for the Association's first formal conference, held in Adelaide in 1983. For a representative instance of his curriculum thinking, see Boomer (1984).
2 First published in 2009, in the Australian curriculum journal *Curriculum Perspectives*.
3 Importantly it qualifies the notion that a book such as this, addressed to 'key figures', is simply an individualist, subject-centred view of history and innovation.
4 Similar initiatives were evident in other Australian states in this period, notably South Australia; in this latter regard, see the chapters by Alan Reid and Jim Dellitt in Yates et al. (2011), which explicitly point to Boomer's influence on that state's characteristic yoking together of social justice and progressive education.
5 In this regard, see in particular "Negotiation Revisited" (Boomer, 1988c) and "Negotiating the Curriculum Reformulated" (Boomer, 1992a).
6 In this regard, see the earlier Schools Council Project (UK) which Nancy Martin coordinated, on writing and learning across the curriculum 11–16 (Martin et al., 1976), as an important precedent. Boomer is acknowledged there as one of several "scholars from overseas who worked with us for long periods of time" (p. 5).
7 Writing a few years after the original publication of his 'manifesto', he asserted: "I would now like to write a book on 'Negotiating the Hidden Curriculum' in which I would complicate the quite simplistic mono-dimensional view of power projected in *Negotiating the Curriculum*" (Boomer, 1988c, p. 171).
8 The most explicit and elaborated account of how Boomer came to understand the concept of power is available in Boomer and Torr (1987) – including his views on the (relative) power of the individual. As he wrote (drawing in part on Foucault), "infinitesimal as it may be, each individual action does change the balance of power" (Boomer & Torr, 1987, p. 3).
9 As he also noted: "*Negotiating the Curriculum* oversimplifies the question of power and largely ignores the negotiation of affection" (Boomer, 1988c, p. 172). He was pointing here to a growing awareness of the significance of affect, and also of desire, in curriculum and teaching.
10 Note Boomer's observations on 'powerlessness' in relation to 'positional power'; he was referring specifically here to teachers in relation to the superordinate figures in their working lives (principals, etc.), but he was also keenly sensitive to larger systemic pressures working on school leaders and others.
11 It should be noted that Boomer himself introduced the notion of 'non-negotiables' – that is, there are always some things which are simply given, whether legislated or else required, in one way or another, and which accordingly need to be worked with, or around. This became all the more significant in ensuing decades, with the inexorable movement towards greater and tighter regulation. It is an important point, however, because it points to the limits of negotiation – and also to Boomer's keen awareness of this. It also counters those criticisms which see negotiation as simply open-ended, overly optimistic, and essentially unrealistic.
12 It may be that the term itself is specific to Australia – it was certainly the term in common usage in the late 70s, when I started teaching, and remained so for quite some time subsequently. See, e.g., Howie (2005).
13 It should be stressed that this applies as much to teachers, as learners, as it does to students.
14 As Reid (2013, p. 43) observes of "Boomer's own 'seven-column' approach", it should be acknowledged that "[t]here are many good frameworks available to help us program"; nonetheless his model has proved particularly useful, particularly in teacher education.
15 This is appropriately linked with Kieran Egan's (1986) work on 'teaching as story-telling' (cf. Reid, 2013, p. 43). In this regard, bearing in mind students as well as teachers,

the following is worth noting: "A story is only completed in the reception of it, as individuals try to make meaning from what they have read or heard, sometimes reacting in radically discrepant ways to the words they have encountered, often by telling their own stories in response" (Doecke & Mirhosseini, 2023, p. 78). This links to Boomer's (1992c, p. 33) observation that curriculum can be "described and comprehended fully only in retrospect", i.e., in the stories generated afterwards, in and after reflection.

16 A further consideration, not developed here, is *resistance*: teachers and other parties might well decide to resist working within the logic and frames of national curriculum and even seek to re-articulate it, at least to some degree. Howie (2006) for instance refers to programming as one way that teachers at the local level might exercise agency and resist "attempts to limit the control [they] have over the nature and effect of [their] work" (p. 234) – "In our programming", he contends, "we write our professional selves and the subject into being" (p. 234).

17 The key point here is that the classroom *matters*, as a significant practice-ontological site.

18 Note, in particular, what is referred to as the *Didaktik* triangle, bringing together teacher, student, and 'content'.

19 See Wells (1995), an important reference-point for understanding curriculum-as-negotiation, as it happens. Wells notes various misconceptions in educational thinking, including "the highly individualistic conception of the learner that undergirds the 'transmissionary' ideology, as Lemke [pers. com.] so aptly terms it" (p. 238). This is akin to what Mayher (1990) calls 'commonsense education' – note Mayher's endorsement of curriculum negotiation, within the context of his 'uncommon-sense' view of education and schooling (pp. 263–267).

20 It was in this context too that Boomer linked the noun to the problematic notions of 'design and development', and also 'implementation', and to the "conceptual separation of curriculum development and teacher development in education systems and schools" (Boomer, 1984, p. 58). It also needs acknowledging that, at that point at least, he was clearly sceptical about the value of (existing) curriculum inquiry as a distinctive enterprise.

21 Given that this chapter is a slightly revised version of one published earlier, in 1982, it indicates both how Boomer understood curriculum, as a *concept*, and his consistent and durable emphasis on curriculum as *practice*.

22 See the following chapter for an elaboration of his point.

23 See Macken-Horarik (2011) for an account of this argument regarding subject English: "the importance of the 'knower code' in the production of a coherent account of disciplinarity in English" (p. 201). The whole 'knowledge' debate is particularly difficult for subject English; for recent work in this regard, see McLean Davies et al. (2023) and Green (2018c).

24 Elliott (1998) continues thus: "At each level representatives of functional groups in our society – teachers, parents, employers, employees – and of appropriate levels of government, would share and negotiate in dialogue their respective visions of educational aims and processes, and attempt to translate the common understandings which emerge into forms of practice that leave room for further debate" (p. 61).

3 'Teacher Power' – On Teachers and Teaching

Garth Boomer was deeply committed to teachers and teaching, and he remained so throughout his career, ranging from his own English classroom to the educational bureaucracy. What would later be called the primacy of practice was in fact his guiding principle, and something he understood implicitly, right from the outset. As he wrote, in what was originally a keynote presented in 1982 at the International Reading Association convention in Chicago: "[T]eacher power is working for literacy in Australia" (Boomer, 1985a, p. 196). This was two years after James Britton declared that the 1980s would be "the decade of the teacher"[1] (Britton, 1982, p. 214) – a statement that can now be seen as a profound historical irony, given how the educational world changed so dramatically in that period, and subsequently. Nonetheless Boomer remained fully committed to such a vision, and strategically so, notwithstanding his recognition that things had indeed changed, and that it had become harder and harder for teachers to, as they say, make a difference, let alone do their job as they themselves conceived it. Policy became ascendant, and then dominant. This was another irony, given Boomer's own movement through (and up) the educational bureaucracy, to the point where he was himself instigating policy. As we have seen, though, he always sought to shape it in accordance with his sense of the profession, at its best, and of professional practice. How then did Boomer represent (English) teachers and teaching?

As a starting-off point, consider the following: "Teachers teach most profoundly what they are at the core. The lasting lesson is the demonstration of the self as it handles its authority and those under its authority" (Boomer, 1988f, p. 31). These are the opening sentences of a keynote that Garth Boomer delivered at a national conference held in Melbourne in 1981. It is in many ways an exemplary statement of Boomer's enduring sense of what it means to be an English teacher, as what might be called a vocation as much as it is a profession. He continued thus: "The self of the *English* teacher demonstrates how to make and take meanings, what to attend to in literature and life, how to make linguistic and life choices, how to be an English teacher and what English is" (p. 31). This is my stepping-off point, then, in this account of Boomer's work and career as a key figure in post-Dartmouth English teaching. Although focused on Australia, his significance is more far-reaching, with relevance and value more generally for English and the language arts in education across the English L1 teaching world. This is notwithstanding the differences as well as the similarities of English teaching in the ex-imperial context.

DOI: 10.4324/9781003374886-3

That teachers "teach most profoundly what they are at the core" is a deeply unfashionable view, it must be admitted. Nonetheless there is something here that warrants attention, even now, especially as we reconsider Boomer's distinctive project as an English educator and as a curriculum leader. This is because his notion of the "lasting lesson" in the practice of English teaching – that the *self* of the English teacher matters, in the exchange(s) of the classroom – remains an important, if rather ambivalent, reference-point. It can be traced back to the Newbolt Report, where the teacher is exhorted to stand before the student, to 'exist', as a Model, an emulable subject. This is by no means necessarily to be understood as an expression of natural authenticity, although this is certainly how it has often been seen. Rather, it is a professional obligation: to *present* oneself (i.e., one's self), as if... At least, this is another way of seeing that statement. That is, this is a mask one must wear, in order to *be* an English teacher, or at least of the sort that matters here. I see this as akin to the notion of the "trusted adult" in the work of the London Writing Research Project (Britton et al., 1975), a notion which was and remains equally problematical and controversial, but which similarly must be recognised in terms of professional obligation, as a strategic role. As Boomer said elsewhere, over a decade later: "Teaching, at the core, is a demonstration of the self, a generous invitation to students to observe how the teacher thinks, feels, understands, solves, and acts" (Boomer, 1993, p. 10). So Boomer's assertion of this demonstration of the self as the "lasting lesson" in post-Dartmouth English teaching is to be seen in such a light. Teachers matter. Teaching matters. And yet his insistence on the 'self' is not necessarily or exclusively to be understood in current-traditional terms, as emanating from a liberal humanist view of human subjectivity, as a particular kind of modernist self-subject. It might be that it can also be seen from a post-humanist, postmodern(ist) perspective, as marking out a *performance*, a strategic construction. The 'self' from such a point of view is itself an artifice, a fiction. There's a balancing-act required here, of course: between one notion of subjectivity and identity, linked to a traditional notion of personhood, and another which emphasises their discursive and constituted nature. However that is worked through, there seems little doubt that taking up a position, speaking from somewhere, in particular ways, is crucial with regard to teacher agency, of the kind that is so clearly at issue here.

A concern with agency and authority is most appropriate. Boomer explicitly and consistently presented a powerful and eloquent case for the importance of teachers and teaching. Perhaps above all else, his work is significant in foregrounding and promoting *pedagogy* as a key organising principle for English teaching, specifically in the post-Dartmouth era. To be clear, it is not that earlier figures in that tradition didn't see teaching as important and even crucial, and indeed what emerges from the historical record is a new awareness of the teacher's role and significance in providing for learners and learning in the context of classrooms. It is, rather, that Boomer focused on this as a crucial matter needing to be addressed, and explicitly. This played out in various ways, as I go on to indicate below.

On 'Teacher Power'

Boomer's vision in this regard is presented here in terms of what is avowedly a metaphor – 'teacher power'. While this isn't one that he developed and deployed himself – at least explicitly – the term does occur in his writing, in various contexts.[2] It is mobilised here as evoking and analogous to the notion of teacher *agency* – teachers as agents. This is intended in the strongest sense, further, to highlight the role and significance of teachers as key agents in education, as 'actors', "highly principled, reflective pragmatic radicals" (Boomer, 1992b, p. 288). The concept of agency is especially important. It is commonly understood within what has been called the structure/agency debate – the tension between affording priority to the structures organising and even determining social life, on the one hand, and what individuals are able to do, in varying accordance with the principle of free will, on the other. In this case, are teachers at the mercy or the command of forces operating beyond them, or are they able to exert a certain degree of counter-pressure, acting and not simply reacting? Teacher agency has been described, accordingly, as how "teachers position themselves politically in relation to change policy, to colleagues and students, and to the wider community" (Priestley et al., 2011, p. 193), and moreover, as "teachers' capacity to act as agents of innovation and change" (p. 194). Boomer was fully aware of this lived tension between structure and agency, freedom and constraint. He was convinced of the need to keep agency firmly on the agenda, and to highlight it, albeit accepting that it was a matter of working always 'against the grain'. This was his version, perhaps, of Gramsci's 'pessimism of the intellect, optimism of the will'. It was consistent too with his evolving understanding of power, and his growing awareness of Foucault and others in this regard. Teachers were to be regarded as intellectuals, moreover, not as technicians. The negotiation project itself, as he saw it, was about "the teacher as 'transformative intellectual'", in Giroux's (1988) sense, "initiating students into new ways of acting in a changing world", with the teacher as "inveterate seeker after wisdom, modelling such an orientation to the world in the enactments of the classroom" (Boomer, 1992b, p. 284). It was in such a context that he introduced his notion of *the pragmatic-radical teacher* (e.g., Boomer, 1999b).

This formulation was introduced as a way of bringing together notions of pragmatism and radicalism, which Boomer clearly saw as important aspects of teachers and teaching, especially in an age of increasing regulation and constraint. It was also a response to new work emerging on critical pedagogy, and influenced by the new sociology of education. Characteristically he rendered radicalism as getting back to "the roots of things, below surfaces and rhetorics" (Boomer, 1992b, p. 276): "My radical is a kind of sceptic or non-conformist in the sense of always searching for alternative interpretations" (p. 276). This included, no doubt, alternatives to established or orthodox views, and dominant, official constructions, and links with his emphasis on reflexivity, although clearly it was also to be seen in the more usual political sense. Balancing this radicalism was a keen awareness of practice and the practical, of operating in an everyday, mundane world with all its nitty-gritty constraints and recalcitrancy – of being pragmatic. "The radical teacher must be a hard-nosed pragmatist keeping alive principles and long-term goals, but having a canny sense of what is achievable, what is not worth the energy and what, however slight, might constitute strategic gain" (p. 280). With more specific regard to English teaching:

> The effective English teacher, I put it to you, is a persisting, struggling, pragmatic radical in the real world. This means knowing about good teaching, having a theorized teaching practice[,] but also being aware of the socio-political context in which teaching operates.
>
> (Boomer, 1993, p. 17)

Such a view placed heavy demands on teachers and teaching, to be sure. But it points to the complexity of pedagogy, too, and its difficulty, and hence its ongoing challenge. This is something that remains relevant, and undeniable, three decades on. In this regard, the case that Boomer presents here remains at once aspirational and inspirational.

How best to understand, to *represent*, teachers and teaching, then? This was central to Boomer's educational project. He was convinced that teaching was all too often misunderstood and misrepresented, overly simplified, stereotyped. How best to respond, then? Characteristically this was to be done by both research and rhetoric – by researching what it is that teachers do, and how they do it, documenting classrooms in action, *and* by mobilising his own considerable rhetorical skills to share the principles of practice. But it was his *conceptualisation* of teachers and teaching that matters most. Once again, Britton's influence, among others (e.g., Barnes) is noticeable. If the new order of things was emphasising and foregrounding learners and learning, what did this mean for teachers and teaching? How might this changed or new role of the teacher be configured and understood? What did it look like?

Representing Teachers and Teaching

In a late paper, Britton (1986) had spoken directly to the challenge of (re)designing English curriculum in accordance with a post-Dartmouth perspective, specifically in relation to pre-service teacher education. In this context, he posed the issue as the need to be less 'teacherly', which here meant being less central to classroom discourse as it plays out – stepping back, as it were. Asked if this meant 'reducing' the role and significance of the teacher, Britton stressed rather that it 'changes' it. "In fact", he wrote, "it is in many ways a more difficult and more complex role than the traditional one". He continued: "We need to know when to stand back and make way for learning to happen – to know when you can stand back, when intervention would in fact be interfering with progress" (Britton, 1986, pp. 156–157). This, he suggested, meant 'listening' – literally but also metaphorically: *not* talking, that is, or refraining from speaking, holding back or holding off, and attuning oneself to what is going on, *for the learner*. He concluded thus: "Don't let anybody suppose that this view of teaching and learning offers the teacher an easier option" (Britton, 1986, p. 158).

This is a particularly neat and succinct statement of post-Dartmouth pedagogy. Whether or not Boomer knew of it, directly, there can be little doubt that he would have recognised its insight and its validity. He was forever trying to find a way of better describing what good teaching looks like, and of better conveying its complexity. "Teaching is a highly complex act", he wrote, "about which we know too little" (Boomer, 1999e, p. 47). The second part of this assertion is equally important here; as he pointed out on various occasions, "education is 'shockingly undocumented'" (p. 40), by which he meant the *practice* of education. This may be as true now as it was then. The task of 'representing' teaching and teachers was one that he took on readily, in his own fashion. This ranged, representatively, from his exploration of what he called the "secret service", in asking the question "What are teachers up to?", playing off the several senses in which that expression might work (Boomer, 1999e), to his prescient essay on professional practice and teacher education (Boomer, 1999f), both of which were written in the late 1980s context of sweeping policy changes in education and schooling, with challenging implications for classroom and teachers. Both papers warrant some discussion here.

The first ("What Are Teachers Up To? Speculating About the Secret Service") opens with the observation that "teaching is probably the most private of all professions and... teaching itself is therefore in many respects a secret service" (Boomer, 1999e, p. 38). In an account that draws in Tracey Kidder's bestselling *Amongst Schoolchildren* (1989), Donald Schön's work on professional practice (1983), and Larry Cuban's historical study of educational change (1984), Boomer argues for a re-assessment of the frames and constraints acting on teachers and teaching. What has changed, over time, if anything other than the 'cosmetic'? What makes for the regularity of classroom practice and the persistence of the recitation?[3] Why has so much remained the same – despite all the undoubted advances in research and theory? (In this respect, of course, he is reflecting on his own change and reform initiatives.) Teaching *is* difficult. Drawing on Kidder, he describes how much teaching is complicated by everything else that is going on, in students' lives and communities, and beyond, always impacting on the teacher's ostensibly primary focus on 'learning':

> [T]he bottom line is that teaching cannot be a pure act of instruction, careless of the human condition of the students. To be connecting with upwards of twenty psyches and wills (not to mentions won'ts) over extended periods is a taxing business.
>
> (p. 42)

Elsewhere he writes memorably that teachers are "continually at war with *contexts*, trying to make them hospitable to their intentions" (Boomer, 1988e, p. 196).

Boomer's realism about the field and the profession is very clear. Teachers vary in their levels and degrees of engagement and commitment, their tenacity and their willingness to keep putting themselves on the line.

[O]ut there, in the secret service, there *are* teachers who are hungry for new ideas, innovation, adventure. These are the ones who tend to join professional associations, attend conferences, undertake further study, or simply remain professionally vigilant for new insights. They will find their own ways to keep themselves 'fresh' as teachers.

(p. 43)[4]

Others ("not to be sneered at") may not go so far, but remain professionally active all the same, albeit in a more constricted way: "They tend to be the silent majority of the secret service, competent, pragmatic, reliable and 'safe'" (p. 43). Even so, he suggests that this reluctance to go beyond a certain point may be for lack of opportunity as much as anything else, and perhaps an inadequate invitation to do and be more. This may be the other side of being pragmatic, then: a quite understandable concern not to expose oneself to risk, or censure.

The other paper ("The Helping Hand Strikes Again: On Language, Learning and Teaching") works off an aphorism attributed to John Holt: 'the helping hand strikes again'. This is yet another an image of teaching in the conventional, common-sense mode, against which Boomer wants to set a counter-image, or perhaps it is another imaginary – the post-Dartmouth teacher, a figure which must be now re-imagined anew. The impulse for teachers to step in, help out, take over, fill the gap, etc., is thoroughly ingrained, and it must be resisted. That impulse stems from a perceived sense of the inadequacy of the Other, a necessary (i.e., 'natural') deficit view. Teachers tend to extend a helping hand far too soon, he suggests, even though with the best of intentions. Teacher educators do the same, along with most other parties surrounding the teacher and proffering advice and calling for change – the research and development 'business'. Boomer's interest here is in "examining the helpfulness or otherwise of those who stand somewhat outside teaching and generate theories, insights, protocols and methods" (Boomer, 1999f, p. 24). He explicitly situates this account within the context of recent debates in the field, including the then current 'process/genre' debate, but also other key initiatives and developments in language education and English teaching, including his own work on negotiating the curriculum. His concern here is to "place language and learning in a wider setting than it is usually given" (p. 24).

The paper itself is an exploration of teaching as (reconceptualised) professional practice. Drawing on Schön and others, including most notably Barnes and also, more implicitly, Stenhouse, he presents a rich and challenging view of teachers and teaching in full accordance with what will later be described as *the primacy of practice thesis*. In this context he highlights the notion of 'knowing-in-practice', of practice knowledge-in-the-making. "What is the kind of knowing in which competent practitioners engage?", he cites Schön in asking. From such a stance he outlines a view of teachers and teaching in terms of the interplay of practice (or 'practice-ing'), science and artistry, beyond technique and (technical) rationality. This is to propose "a new science of teaching" (p. 30), a new *living* science, predicated on privileging the practical and investing teachers and teaching with a new and compelling significance. Teaching is too complex, he suggests, for any single-vision explanatory and appreciative systems that might be available, and classrooms-in-action must be seen as chaotic, in a certain manner of speaking as 'messes' which need to be 'managed', drawing on diverse and different resources. This is a call for humility, then, and for reflexivity. Practising teachers are best conceived as 'managers of messes', as "managing messes" (p. 25), making them work and as best as possible, thinking in and through action, and working as much as anything else through improvisation, intuition and (ir)rationality. Above all else, this is a *proficiency* view of teachers and teaching – and this, at a time when teachers were increasingly seen as 'objects' of intervention. We shall return to this paper later.

English Teaching as Art *and* Science? – or, 'The Wonder of Ourselves…'

One of Boomer's most interesting essays is "English Teaching: Art and Science" (1988h), first presented as a keynote address at the 1984 NCTE annual conference in Detroit and later published in the book emerging from the IFTE seminar held at Michigan State the same year (Tchudi, 1985).[5] It quickly became a major reference-point for his distinctive vision of the field, certainly in Australia. The title itself would have intrigued. A year earlier, in 1983, Boomer had addressed another national English teaching conference, this time in Canada, presenting a paper entitled "Towards a Science of English Teaching" (Boomer, 1983). There, he acknowledged the apparent incongruity of associating English teaching with 'science', relating it to what he saw as a much weaker formulation – 'the principles and practice of English teaching' – before asserting that his proper focus was indeed on working towards a what might justly be described as a 'science' of (English) teaching. This was consistent with his growing interest at this time on becoming more systematic and explicit about knowledge, both that of the classroom and that of the profession. Regarding the latter in particular, he began to call for the *codification* of knowledge, as a way of making it explicit and accessible.

Elsewhere he wrote: "I want to argue that to assist teachers' liberation it would be helpful if we began by codifying and explaining, if possible, what actually happens in the act of teaching" ("Teaching Against the Grain" – Boomer, 1988g, p. 182). Further: "If teaching were codified, there would be the possibility of deliberate experimentation in order to question the established codes and conventions. The science cannot be advanced because we cannot see the frontier" ("Teaching Against the Grain", p. 190).

While the "Art and Science" paper needs to be read in this context, it also picks up on another preoccupation on Boomer's part. This was the need he felt, firstly, to fully and appropriately acknowledge teachers and teaching, and to represent them as best he could; and secondly, to point to the manifest inadequacies of much academic endeavour in this regard (including that which, he acknowledged, he himself was much indebted to, and in which he was immersed). "Even when people like the great synthesiser James Britton bring together philosophers, linguists, psychologist and sociologists", he wrote, "the offering to teachers is relatively narrow" (Boomer, 1999f, p. 31).

And so it is for research and scholarship more generally, *despite* its insights and advances, and more generally its 'helpfulness'. We will see later how he perceived the role and significance of action research and practitioner enquiry, given all this.

The "Art and Science" paper introduced 'Mrs Bell' to the English teaching world.[6] This was one of a number of such 'portraits', as it happens. Around about the same time, he introduced 'Mr Flanders' and 'Ms Mayler', which were deliberately linked to other "[f]ictional portraits of teachers", other "public-domain fictional or semi-autobiographical images of 'good' and 'bad' teachers" (Green, 2003a, p. 8). This was Boomer's way of drawing on his own largely informal, anecdotal research, drawing on his experience as well as public debate and scholarship, to generate *and* interrogate images of teaching, its mythologies, fantasies, and stereotypes. The paper itself combined this with a more conventional research practice, in the participant-observation mode, although this would appear to have been conducted relatively informally. The work in this regard can be seen as a form of curriculum and cultural criticism, somewhat in the tradition of Thomas Barone and others, and still scarcely valued or understood.[7] The aim was to work with – and on – representations as 'texts'. 'Mrs Bell' was a fiction, then, a composite figure, an experienced (Australian) English teacher working with a Year 10 class of 15-year-olds, in the context of a curriculum unit of study organised around a novel. These then are 'triangulated', although largely implicitly, briefly synthesised, and then offered to the attuned reader. . Commentary and conclusions are then drawn from all of this. A claim to authenticity is made:

> We who have been teachers, too, recognise it [i.e., this account] as authentic. This archaeological exercise reminds us of treasures we tend to bury and forget; things we know but do not speak of when we write about the art and science of our own teaching; perhaps so taken-for-granted that we de-value them.
>
> (Boomer, 1988h, p. 85)

This is knowledge and experience that all too often remains unrecognised, or tacit.

Mrs Bell is described as "a da Vinci and a Galileo" (Boomer, 1988h, p. 88) – an artist *and* a scientist. But there is also technique involved, and craft: "Implicit in any art or science is technology and skill in the manipulation of media" (p. 93). This is something acquired through practice, and repetition as well as reflection. It is the teacher who brings it all together, in interaction with her students (and also the situation itself, in all its dynamic materiality). She is described, memorably, as "poly-attentive" – although how that capacity comes about, developmentally, might still be something to ponder. Moreover, she is actively engaged, fully on task:

> With one part of her mind's-eye on the imagined outcomes, she must read with feeling and sensitivity from the novel, while sensing whether she has engaged the class, knowing how much time she has left and remaining ready to break off her explanation at any time according to a judgement of whether this is necessary or whether it would intrude on the spell of the story. In

James Britton's terms, she must have both a global and piecemeal awareness of what is happening. *The technician, the scientist and the artist work together.*
(p. 97; my added emphasis)

There is a story being told here, a narrative unfolding. It is an experiment in representation: a classroom in action, over the duration of a curriculum unit. It is described as a "picture [painted] of infinite embeddedness" (p. 89):

> The teaching moment is set within the teaching sequence, set within a particular classroom of a particular school in a particular socio-political context at a particular moment in history. The participants can cause infinite variations from moment to moment, each coming from a distinct and complex setting, and each interpreting the moment differently.
> (p. 89)

The story of Mrs Bell and her students, in *that* classroom, is presented finally, as a demonstration of good English teaching – representing the practice of English teaching, complex as that is – in itself. But it is also a *celebration* of English teaching, and of English teachers, an invitation to wonder anew at what is being achieved here. As it concludes: "I hope that we can all recognise in Mrs Bell the wonder of ourselves" (Boomer, 1988h, p. 118).[8]

Well-received as it was, and indeed has continued to be, with intermittent re-publishing, the paper nonetheless has attracted criticism, and understandably so. It reads somewhat naively now, and perhaps as rather idealistic, even romantic, and certainly in various ways dated. Nonetheless, the paper richly announced Boomer's distinctive project in this respect, and his deep commitment to teachers and teaching. It is still rare to find such accounts in the literature. Re-published in the late 1990s, in *English in Australia*, it provoked varying responses. One commentator was particularly strong in his criticism, seeing the paper as both inadequate and unfair to the real-world struggle of English teachers, and as marking simply "a spectator's legacy":

> In my view, celebration of the kind of qualities I ... identified above has led to a number of pedagogic and structural approaches within schools that have often been less productive than those which they replaced because they rely for their success on an unusual talent or skill generally possessed by only a very small proportion of the teaching profession.
> (Howes, 1998, pp. 27–28)

For Howes, Boomer's influence was "destructive" (p. 27). Another pointed to its heroic individualism, its romanticism, its indulgence, and its rhetorical flourish, especially noting its excessive use of metaphors (McClenaghan, 1998). These views can perhaps be seen as immersed in the professional present of that time and a certain ideology of language and the practical – and as needing a larger historical perspective. A third commentator, also a teacher, wrote: "In this famous essay,

Boomer sets out to tell us about what Mrs Bell had been able to do with her class. And this is something that we are not used to hearing" (Noden, 1998, p. 6). Ironically, calls were made for a more measured, realistic engagement with professional practice, citing Schön's encouragement of work more attuned to, and immersed in, what he famously described as the 'swamplands', and the 'messy' nature of practitioners' everyday work-lives – unaware that this was precisely the territory Boomer was himself exploring, from the mid-1980s on.

Perhaps more pertinent here, what such criticisms suggest is the need to learn how best to read texts such as this one, both with and against the grain. This involves, in the first instance, re-contextualising such a paper, produced in the early 1980s, in a particular discursive environment, and re-produced on various other occasions, intermittently, after that. There is an important sense in which the 'text' becomes something different over the course of that reading history, which is all the more interesting when it is linked intertextually to other papers that Boomer presented in this period. For instance, the short piece "Ten Strategies for Good Teaching" (Boomer, 1982a) presents ten "general principles or broad strategies", as a kind of 'grammar' pertaining to "the framework of a negotiated curriculum" (p. 119).[9] Succinct and beautifully written, it is a good early example of Boomer's characteristic use of the list form, seen again in the 'Mrs Bell' essay, for instance. One such strategy is "connecting", glossed thus:

> The more richly a teacher can spin a tapestry of metaphor and analogy into a 'thick' redundant text of thinking about something new, the more likely it is that students will find a way in. If students are encouraged to spin out reciprocally their own webs of anecdote, metaphor and analogy, it is less likely that some will remain outside the next text. The art of generating apt analogy and metaphor is central to the ... teacher's task.
>
> (Boomer, 1982a, p. 120)

Teaching is understood here, crucially, as making (good) connections with learners/readers. What might be seen as more or less ornamental and perhaps even indulgent in the account of Mrs Bell and her English classroom – the rich use of metaphors, etc. – is, rather, a pedagogic device, and this is what is being demonstrated in the essay.

Similarly, the relatively late paper "How to Make a Teacher", first delivered at the NCTE Spring Conference in Washington in 1992 and published a year later (Boomer, 1993), is offered as another representation of English teachers and English teaching. This was not a conventional academic presentation, however; it was a *performance*. This time, instead of attempting to portray the scene of English teaching, to play it out as it were, this was a presentation of "seven essences, distillations from a lifetime of thinking about teaching and learning, each essence going to the core" (p. 5) – seven principles that make, in and through practice, for what he saw as good English teaching. These were, in summary, *provocation, negotiation, demonstration, transformation, reflection, passion/desire,* and *pragmatism*. Further terms are introduced along the way, including "intention" ("the key to powerful learning"), "disequilibrium", "praxis", "selective inattention" (citing Schön) and others, in a presentation that is clearly echoing other papers, quite deliberately and sometimes almost archly so. Hence:

> The metaphor is, if you like, a form of grappling hook drawing the novel and unexamined into the realm of the known. Interestingly, the more perverse or bizarre the connection the more powerfully an idea or insight may be consolidated and defined.
>
> (Boomer, 1993, p. 12)

The paper concludes with the revelation of "an eighth essence, PERFORMANCE, but that's a story for another day!" – thus ending what has clearly been itself a performance, with imaginary interlocutors and commentators and Boomer himself wearing different hats at different points, literally... What we are left with, finally, is a weaving of the representational, the performative and the pedagogic, but also, along with a powerful sense of his actively theorised vision of teachers and teaching, a new reflexive element, and it is to this we now turn.

English Teaching as Post-Epic Pedagogy

Perhaps Boomer's single most powerful statement in this context is the paper "Literacy: The Epic Challenge Beyond Progressivism", first presented as a conference keynote in 1989 (Boomer, 1999g).[10] Produced at a time when, as he explicitly acknowledged, he was increasingly detached from the grounded world of schools and classrooms as practical sites, in this paper he set out to confront and challenge the current orthodoxy regarding so-called 'progressive' teachers and teaching. In doing so, he was quick to include himself in that grouping, noting his own professional and intellectual history and his role in promoting certain discourses identified with the label 'progressivism', which here has been linked to post-Dartmouth English teaching. As he wrote: "I am an idealistic 'progressive' trying to become a more pragmatic 'radical'" (Boomer, 1999g, p. 84). Further, he recognised at the outset that he was addressing what was at best a narrow selection from the broader professional constituency, describing them as "practising or potential boundary riders", and as "modern teachers, progressive teachers, enquiring teachers" (p. 83), representing at most around 10% of that larger grouping. This is, in itself, a difficult issue: the problem of 'avant-garde-ism', as it might be called, or the minority uptake of leading-edge ideas and arguments in the field. It was something he was increasingly aware of, as a long-time advocate for change and reform: the sheer difficulty of large-scale, sustainable mobilisation, and the dangers and seductions associated with associated movements and initiatives. In that regard, he noted that "progressivism has now taken the high rhetorical ground in literacy education in Australia, something that is not so in other Western countries" (p. 84), with systems and departments across the country endorsing 'progressive' lines of thinking, to the point of now being a new orthodoxy, in policy if not in practice. "I am therefore led to ask", he wrote, "why our rhetoric has not gripped in the classroom" (p. 87). This was his starting point then for the current paper, as a deliberate intervention into the prevailing mindset, at least as he saw it, very much thinking *against* the grain.

The paper itself explicitly sets 'progressivism' against 'radicalism', as two rather schematic organising principles, but also very much a strategic opposition, rhetorically and conceptually. The first is readily recognisable, and indeed can be referenced back in various ways (although not entirely or straightforwardly) to 'Mrs Bell' and other like figures. The 'progressive' teacher is presented as "one who is seeking to develop personally and professionally by considering and, after reflection, acting upon new insights and understandings of the art and science of teaching" (p. 84) – albeit always within limits. A "believer in the notion of human perfectibility", s/he works in a principled way to achieve both student learning and social justice, although in practice the former tends to have effective priority, with his/her focus on the individual. S/he is essentially liberal in his/her worldview. Against this is set the so-called 'radical' teacher, someone who is more politically active and aware, who doesn't want to accept the social world as it is, and indeed wants to change it, and make it better:

> To be radical means to go beneath manifestations and events for causes and connections; not to remain enthralled by glittering surfaces. To be radical is to be threatening: because you question the very basis of society; because you try to transform or make opaque, transparent habit and common sense. It also implies some form of solidarity with fellow, like-minded, radicals committed to transformative action; and hence a tendency to be less individualistic than the progressive.
> (p. 84)

Yet this is also someone who has learnt to be pragmatic, who knows how to read the situation in which s/he finds him/herself, and how to work strategically within it – indeed this figure is more appropriately described as a *pragmatical-radical* practitioner, as adumbrated and elaborated elsewhere (e.g., Boomer et al., 1992). This is in fact what he has been moving towards, over the past decade at least, moving "further along the path of construing a new kind of postmodern, post-progressive teacher: the pragmatic radical – or, to be more evocative, the EPIC teacher" (p. 91). Ten years earlier, he had proposed that students be taught to "read the whole curriculum" (Boomer, 1988d), and to consider the curriculum as itself a text, something that might be read against (as well as with) the grain.

> Curriculum is never 'natural', or inevitable. This is an important point, as I see it. Many students don't question the curriculum; it is simply there to be taken, they receive it, and they never question that it is made by someone.
> (Boomer, 1988d, p. 154)[11]

Because it is 'made', moreover, it can be 'un-made', or changed. That incubating idea, as he puts it, has now emerged in the notion of a new generative metaphor: teaching as performance, and curriculum as theatre.

Hence his interest in developing a Brechtian perspective on education and schooling, and more specifically English teaching and literacy education. This had been brewing for quite some time, as noted, but crystallised here, in the "Epic Challenge" paper.[12] It explicitly engages the concept of 'epic theatre', associated with the German playwright and poet Bertolt Brecht and as discussed by Walter Benjamin, the German literary scholar.[13] This was conceptualised in deliberate contrast to 'naturalistic theatre', as the more mainstream, orthodox form.[14] Rather than creating an illusion of reality, a "charming" reality-effect, "Epic Theatre deliberately draws attention to itself as theatre. It cultivates what Brecht called a *verfremdungeffekt* – more popularly translated as the famous 'alienation effect'" (Boomer, 1999g, p. 91) – or, as Boomer notes, "the 'estrangement effect'". The aim of epic theatre is to challenge and estrange the audience, thereby provoking them to *think*. "Epic theatre casts doubt upon the notion that theatre is entertainment" (Benjamin, 1983, p. 9). Rather than immersion and astonishment, or indeed entertainment, what is sought is *interruption*; the work is conceived as an intervention, a radical de-naturalisation.

> Epic theatre is definitely not naturalistic. It is stylised, self-conscious, and overtly intentional. The audience, whilst critically estranged, is nonetheless pressured to see the familiar in a new light, to question old constructs, and to be shocked (but not surprised).
>
> (Boomer, 1999g, p. 91)

In similar fashion, what might be called 'epic pedagogy' is set against 'naturalistic' education. From the perspective of 'progressive' pedagogy,

> [t]he curriculum becomes almost like doing what comes 'naturally'. Children are surprised, delighted, entertained, and engrossed. And thus, they are manipulated – because the curriculum is not, in fact, natural but, rather, *constructed*, and the teacher, in seeming not to design, has palpable designs on the learners.
>
> (p. 91)

The problem is this is neither acknowledged nor made explicit; it is caught up in what Boomer elsewhere calls the "complicity of tact", a liberal reluctance to come clean, to name ugly or unpleasant or more negative things as they are, to leave certain matters unsaid – a politics of the tacit. What might an epic pedagogy look like, then? We have already seen aspects of this in earlier accounts of curriculum negotiation and the pragmatic-radical professional, or at least gestures towards it. Here it is made explicit, and elaborated:

> An Epic Teacher, unlike the naturalistic teacher, would show the students that the curriculum is a construction designed to have certain effects on them. He or she would be continually taking students behind the set of his or her own theatre of performance, to see the scaffolding and the construction

technologies. The Epic Teacher would assiduously cultivate an estrangement effect, both with respect to his/her own views and with respects to the ideas and knowledge being promulgated. The students would be expected to be engaged and yet critical; moved, and yet gently sceptical. The teacher would work dialectically to confront the values of the learners and also to confront and gently undermine him/herself. The classroom itself, as a community or sub-culture, would be rendered problematic. The teacher would be overtly didactic. Whereas the naturalistic teacher would manipulate by deceptions or 'silences', the Epic Teacher would manipulate explicitly and self-consciously.

(Boomer, 1999g, p. 91)

It is important to bear in mind that there have been similar passages previously and elsewhere. For instance, from 1981:

Consider the curriculum as a kind of Hollywood western town teaching set. What we should be doing, I believe, is saying, 'Come behind here and I'll show you how it works'. By that I mean, letting students into one's seemingly magic curriculum tricks, or, to put it another way, leaving uncovered the footprints so often carefully dusted over. The God in the machine is really only an experienced mortal and it would be a relief to so many tribal sinners to know it. So many vain sacrifices and fruitless rain dances would thus be rendered unnecessary.

(Boomer, 1988d, pp. 161–162)

In 1992, the point is made thus:

Most teaching is somewhat analogous to naturalistic theatre which is effective by being so enthralling or capturing the audience that they suspend disbelief entering into the constructed world of the drama as if it were natural. Brechtian theatre operates on the principle of setting up *patently constructed* images of life as mirrors for critique and evaluation.

(Boomer, 1992b, p. 285)

The passage continues:

A Brechtian-type classroom will similarly present the curriculum as a construct which can be critiqued and evaluated by the students. This may be an engrossing and disturbing classroom but it is not enthralling. The naturalistic classroom presents as TRUTH. The epic classroom, as I call it, presents as a laboratory for the scrutiny of alleged truth.

(p. 285)

The aim is to make "the teaching and the curriculum *opaque*" (p. 285), no longer transparent, a window on reality, something that one simply looks through. Ironically the medium itself becomes invisible. What is being suggested here is the need to problematise the pervasive *realism* of much educational thinking and the action associated with it. Hence the significance of the brief mention here of figures such as William Doll, Henry Giroux, and Patti Lather, introducing not just a more socially critical perspective but also, more specifically, the 'postmodern' as a frame of reference, which was a strong and influential line of educational scholarship at that time. Boomer presents this under the heading 'postmodern challenges' (p. 89): "Dense and somewhat impermeable, but nonetheless intriguing, postmodernist thinkers are challenging the very foundations of the present paradigms of all disciplines, *including education*" (p. 89; my added emphasis). This is the intellectual, cultural, and political context then of his explorations of a "postmodern, post-progressive" pedagogy, which he readily conceded were uncertain and still perhaps insufficiently assimilated. It was a particular slant on the postmodern too that he was working his way towards, as indicated by his tentative reflections on holist philosophy and new forms of organicism in his "Dancing Lessons" essay (Boomer, 1988b), which can be seen now to have various connections with the spiritual turn in the later Moffett, as well as his comments here, in particular, on Doll's distinctive account of 'postmodern curriculum' and new mathematico-scientific thinking (see also Doll, 1993).

Boomer goes on to outline a cluster of epigraphic features of what he presents as the 'Epic' teacher, followed by those to be associated with the 'pragmatic radical', which is perhaps too schematic a move, because the effect of doing so might be seen to identify the two, more or less, or as presenting them as effectively isomorphic. That would be unfortunate, and misleading. This is because what such a reading closes down is the possibility of a more strategic interpretation. The initial oppositional interplay of the 'progressive' and the 'radical' morphs into that between the 'progressive' and the 'epic', which becomes the actual focus of Boomer's argument, itself an exercise in dialectical thinking. This brings the 'progressive' and the 'epic' together, as a form of 'thesis' and 'antithesis' – but without any subsequent move to a transcending 'synthesis'. Rather, what emerges here is to be seen as a new formulation, named here as the 'pragmatic-radical', a third term, which draws on both of those earlier terms and goes beyond them. This is the sense that Boomer evokes in writing:

> I do not see the pragmatic radical as a *displacement* of the progressive so much as *an advanced form*. There is not necessary need or reason, I believe, to abandon the language learning theories underpinning progressivism, but there is a need to set these understandings in a wider, bolder context.
> (p. 93; my added emphasis)

Seen in this light, the essay can be recognised as a *thought-experiment*, literally. It plays out an argument, as itself an instance of epic pedagogy, inviting its audience and its readership, its constituency, to think against the grain – the grain of the self, as much as anything else. And there is no doubt that it was indeed confrontational, and deliberately, even programmatically so. It is worth bearing in mind, at this point, the observation that Boomer made elsewhere, about "[t]eachers teach[ing] most profoundly what they are at the core", with the "lasting lesson" being "the demonstration of the self as it handles its authority and those under its authority" (Boomer, 1988f, p. 31). Can this be seen as another version, then, of that call for a radical reflexivity on the part of the profession, even at its best? A matter, that is, of problematising the 'self' of English teaching, and its self-understanding, without however thereby rejecting it?

A few final comments on this essay, which is certainly one of his most thought-provoking and controversial. First, a case can be made that what emerges is what might be called a *post-epic pedagogy*, or the rudiments of this, at least. This is to register this particular essay as one attempt to outline what pedagogy might look like in postmodern times and conditions – a strategic articulation of the 'postmodern' and the 'epic' (bearing in mind, of course, that Brecht himself was quintessentially a modernist figure...). Hardly anyone else was doing this at the time, certainly in English teaching. Indeed, the case can be made that the pedagogy imagined here is not so much for classrooms as it is for conferences such as that at which the "Epic" paper was first presented – that the conference was itself a scene of pedagogy. After all, the conference address was now where Boomer principally did his 'teaching', and as he readily acknowledged he was operating at some distance from actual schools and the daily work of classroom teachers. In yet another sense of this, what emerges from this exercise is something like an *(in)visible pedagogy* – one combining the 'visible' (i.e. the 'epic') and the 'invisible' (i.e. the 'naturalistic'), in a new logic of both/and *and* neither/nor. This might be still worth thinking about in dialogue with work such as that of Gregory Ulmer, an American cultural scholar, who draws extensively on Derrida and others (Ulmer, 1985). An (in)visible pedagogy[15] here would be one which both deployed all the resources of so-called progressivist education and deconstructed them, re-working them, re-articulating and rethinking them – thinking them again, and anew.

Something else to take into account is the risk involved in working as Boomer did in this essay, so provocatively. As one (supportive) commentator observed, "to mount arguments which are too far removed from current practice, no matter what perceived levels of 'progressiveness' marked this space, was to invite responses that ranged from outright denial to apathy" (Corcoran, 1998, p. 114). Boomer was clearly working "far removed from current practice" here. The reaction was considerable, and not for the first time Boomer was heavily criticised, and accused of betraying the cause. He acknowledged this in the Postscript he wrote for the 1999 version, with its relayed presentation for a 'Whole Language' conference held in Niagara Falls in 1992. By this time, he had experienced something of the almost evangelical fervour of the Whole Language movement, especially in North America, as well as its widespread take-up in Australia, in one form or another, and he had become more and more sceptical, as might be expected. As he wrote: "After this Darwin piece, I certainly had my critics, and, to an extent I had not fully anticipated, the debate still continues" (Boomer, 1999g, p. 95). One such critic, he noted, "took me to task ... in what I assessed to be a largely *ad hominem* plaint, characterising me as a kind of 'traitor' whose mind had been befuddled with academic abstractions".[16] "He was wrong, in my view", he wrote, "to imply that I had suddenly fallen prey to 'false consciousness', although I now know he was not alone in this judgement" (p. 95). This kind of critical commentary was indeed symptomatic, then and perhaps even now. If the case that is made here is correct, he was misread, then and now, and the quality of his intervention, his thought-experiment, is still under-appreciated.

Teachers as Researchers, or Becoming Our Own Experts

In a keynote delivered at the Sydney IFTE conference in 1980, Boomer wrote the following:

> One of the most exciting advances of the past ten years has been the growth in 'action research' – teachers recording, documenting and reflecting on the life of their own classrooms. Slowly and significantly this will change the balance of story-telling power. Metaphors are being exchanged and evaluated: 'It's a fine metaphor, Professor Bernstein, but it doesn't fit my classroom as neatly as you seem to suggest'.
> (Boomer, 1988i, p. 26)

Serving also as a succinct expression of what is called here 'teacher power', this statement indicates a particularly significant feature of Boomer's work as a whole: his commitment to collective, collaborative activity on the part of English teachers and the profession more generally. He was surely referring to initiatives and undertakings such as the 'Becoming Our Own Experts' project (Eyers & Richmond, 2012), operating in London in the late 1970s, as well as the grassroots work associated with the London Institute of Education and the London Association of Teachers of English (LATE), which later morphed into a national association (National Association of Teachers of English; NATE), which he would have encountered first-hand in his study-leave period in the UK. Another influence was undoubtedly that of Lawrence Stenhouse and his work on teachers as researchers, and his view of "curriculum research and development" as "based on the study of classrooms" and accordingly "rest[ing] on the work of teachers" (Stenhouse, 1975, p. 143). Boomer was active in this regard himself, participating in and overseeing language-and-learning work in South Australia in the mid-1970s and extending this to the national context subsequently. As he wrote, this work "pioneered and confirmed action research by teachers as a means of professional development", although "[b]ecause the term 'action research' was daunting to many would-be participants, the 'language across the curriculum' project preferred to use the term 'teacher inquiry'" (Boomer, 1985c, p. 121). Importantly this points to direct, organic links between the language-and-learning movement and action research, the latter becoming increasingly significant in Australian educational research in the 1980s and beyond. It wasn't incidental or at all gestural, in 1992, for Boomer to put "An Invitation to Action Research" as the subtitle for his "Curriculum Composing and Evaluating" chapter (Boomer, 1992c).[17] This emphasis on teachers as (action) researchers was a constant feature of his project, in fact, and from the very beginning.

Hence it is worth looking at the paper "Addressing the Problem of Elsewhereness: A Case for Action Research in Schools" (Boomer, 1985b), originally presented in 1981 at an invitational symposium on action research held at Deakin University. It introduces firstly a working distinction between what is described as 'big R' and 'little r' research, thereby acknowledging the then current-traditional relationship between researchers (principally academics) and practitioners, as more than simply a technical division of labour. As he put it, perhaps reflecting wryly on his own situation, "[r]esearch in education is a postgraduate luxury" (p. 123). Research, properly conceived, is "self-conscious and deliberate" learning. Researchers in this sense – scientists, mathematicians, writers, etc. –

> continually seek out solutions to problems and test their findings in order to be what they are. Their trades, while differentiated at the surface level, are at base the same. They are professional generators of hypotheses and seekers of solutions.
>
> (p. 123)

What about teachers? Clearly "teachers teach science and mathematics and English", and much else:

> To do this they, too, must generate their hypotheses and test them, hypotheses about how to teach the next concept, how best to provide materials, how best to control, how best to arrange and order the syllabus and so on. They are to this extent action researchers in teaching. This is where they have knowledge beyond that of any outside student of education. They are applied educationists. What they are likely to teach students best, then, is what teachers do: how to be taught, how to deal with school, how to be a scholar and so on.

But, as he adds, "usually they do not do this *deliberately and explicitly*" (p. 123; his emphasis). This is Boomer's key point, and it is central to his work more generally, in advocating for teacher agency as a crucial factor in genuine and robust educational reform. Teachers – and students – should become researchers, as absolutely central to their work and time together, in classrooms conceived as "laboratories", or perhaps as workshops (Reid, 1984). This is to see classrooms as sites of systematic and explicit learning, on the part of students, certainly, but also – and importantly – on the part of teachers. Why is it, he wonders, that teachers are so often 'alienated' from "their own craft, the craft of teaching and learning"? This refers to not simply what they *do*, as teachers, their activities, their *practice*, but also its medium, most notably their language, although the body is significant here as well. The challenge is how to bring all this to consciousness, and make it properly and productively reflexive.

This is where the teacher as researcher comes in. This is to undertake, in the first instance, to inquire into what goes on in one's own classroom. The reason for doing so is not simply to understand it – important as that is – but to change it, improve it, make it better; but also, in order to do it better next time. And it is the teacher, as professional practitioner, who arguably is best placed to do this, and with clear interest in doing so. This would be research, or inquiry, that was in Boomer's terms 'owned' by the participants: "By 'owned'", he wrote,

> I mean 'owned' by the person or the group doing the research. This is their *own* research into their *own* problem so that the subsequent action is also 'owned'. The resultant action will be a modification, however minimal, of their *own* behaviour. The research cannot be disowned.
> (p. 124)

The focus is on changing and improving one's own practice. This is how Boomer understands action research, then: "Action research is deliberate, group or personally owned and conducted, solution-oriented investigation" – that is, a form of "deliberate learning" (p. 124). Moreover: "'Action research', as defined, is personally owned learning. It is, if you like, the antithesis of, and antidote to, 'elsewhereness'" (p. 125). There is a ready connection to be made, further, with the notion of research as 'systematic inquiry made public', associated with Stenhouse – especially when Boomer's interest in teachers as writers is factored in.[18]

With this point established, Boomer moves on to make explicit connection with his negotiating-the-curriculum work, with action research so defined – or practitioner inquiry, as such professional activity was later formulated (Campbell & Groundwater-Smith, 2009; Nichols & Cormack, 2017) – central to it. As he writes here:

> I propose that any learning sequence should begin with a negotiation of intentions to the point that both teacher and student intend in the same direction and mutually *own* the curriculum *as jointly planned*. Under this model, the unit of curriculum is itself a piece of action research into learning which can be reflected upon and evaluated by both teacher and student.
> (p. 128)

In this view, teacher programming, as 'composing' rather than 'planning', is at the very least congruent with action research, thus conceived – perhaps even more so when the programme is textualised. Negotiating the curriculum, properly understood, involves not simply curriculum co-construction but also collaborative research, on the part of teachers and students, aimed at making the classroom as productive and fulfilling as possible. This is idealistic, of course, but worth articulating all the same, and hence having available as an image of possibility, a resource for hope. (This is, in fact, an important consideration in revisiting Boomer's overall project.) In a passage that has echoes with other papers we have met here, Boomer writes:

> I contend that the curriculum itself must be problematic for the teachers *and* the students. What shall we teach and learn? How shall we teach and learn it? Why is it worth doing and why are we compelled to do it? What is of such minor significance that it can be told (facts, information, background). What is of such major significance that it must be experienced and investigated in order to be owned?
>
> (pp. 128–129)

These are questions fundamental to pedagogy, and programming. They reach right to the heart of issues of sequence, continuity, and development, of knowledge that matters, of organisation and instruction, of resourcing, and much else. Moreover, questions such as these are the province and the concern not simply of teachers and teaching, Boomer believes, but of students and learners too. This is not so much, in the latter case, that they come to constitute the curriculum, at least in its entirety – although a case can be made that there is value in making at least some of this available for students' formal curriculum work. Matters pertaining to citizenship and democracy come to mind, for instance, or what might be really useful knowledge in an age of climate emergency. The point is, there is particular value in bringing action research of the kind envisaged and imagined here into central consideration, in contemplating professional development and curriculum renewal. This particularly holds for teachers, in the present context. "Action research will bring theory and practice together, *here* in the classroom. Answers will be sought *here* rather than *elsewhere*" (p. 129).

Boomer's essay has been influential, although perhaps less so than might have been the case.[19] It may be best seen in relation to the wider context of his writing, which has been scattered about and sometimes less than carefully or rigorously read, alert to its intertextuality. Readily acknowledging her indebtedness, Comber (2013) revisited it in specific relation to her longstanding interest in teachers as researchers (Comber, 2016), within an action-research framework. As she observed, "[Boomer's] capacity to imagine a different kind of teacher workforce was breathtaking" (p. 55). Action research was central to his vision of teachers and teaching, as she noted:

> Key principles historically associated with action research – its focus on experienced problems, classroom and school-based inquiry processes, teacher action and data-informed change to practice and policy – require both a highly educated and ethical practitioner.
>
> (p. 55)

She pinpoints the *social* implications of such work, observing that action research is neither "neutral" nor "instrumental". "Indeed', she writes, "action research always involves critical analysis of the ways in which current practices impact on different participants. It is always concerned with questions of justice" (p. 55). Or rather, action research of the kind that Comber and Boomer both endorsed – bearing in mind that it has all too often been appropriated for other, more technical, even technocratic ends. It is social also in the sense that, although it begins necessarily with the teacher and his/her own classroom, it ideally and preferably goes beyond that to include collaborative endeavour and teachers working together, in communities of inquiry. It is certainly not an individualistic endeavour, at its best. This is why Comber herself, extending Boomer's legacy, continues to champion teacher-researchers, and argues that "the relationships between teachers and research, teachers and knowledge production, teachers and researchers remain under-investigated" (Comber, 2013, p. 60). He would have welcomed work of this kind. Not only would it change the prevailing social relations – even now – of research and pedagogy, classroom teachers and academic researchers, scholars and practitioners, but it would allow for interruption and the possibility of change in education and schooling more generally, and certainly in educational research and curriculum inquiry.

As it was, Boomer remained committed to the notion of teachers and teaching as absolutely central to the whole enterprise, even in his later work as a senior educational bureaucrat. As he wrote, apropos the controversial move to national profiles and standards in Australian education in the later 1980s: "As I read it, the profiles approach comes out of a strongly teacher-centred, classroom-oriented understanding of how judgement works on a day to day basis in our schools" (Boomer, 1992e, p. 164). His unwavering commitment to this principle is evident too in his comments on the 'Windows on Practice' project in South Australia during this period, which he describes as "premised on the view that teaching practice is overly private, sequestered and unregarded. Teachers will learn best from each other *if given the opportunity*. Failing face-to-face observation, the next best thing is documentation of practice, using print, media and audio-visual media". As he puts it: "The art will be to document, as authentically as possible, how teachers operate in various contexts" (Boomer, 1999e, p. 46). Teachers themselves were to be key actors in this endeavour.

Conclusion

Two points are worth noting. The first is the significance of the concept of *practice*, or rather practice as *concept*, to be more fully and adequately theorised two decades later.[20] Boomer was one of the first to pick this up, however, in his early explorations of 'the practical' and the need to problematise and privilege it. As he wrote:

> we will only privilege the practical if we learn more about how the practical works, in all its complexity, and then set about teaching how to do 'action research' on knowledge-in-practice within the richest frames of reference, rendering all aspects of the act problematic from time to time, including the overarching appreciative system itself.
>
> (Boomer, 1999f, p. 30)

He was proposing an important shift: "[L]anguage education has been at once too narrowly about language and education and too little cognisant of the contested and highly complex act of teaching" (p. 33). As he put it, eloquently and presciently:

> In classrooms the problem of Johnny who never sits down can be as profound as the problem of how to teach Johnny to read. We need to develop much better theories of the practical (including the pragmatics of classroom management) in which to embed our theories of language and learning.
>
> (p. 33)

The second point is the focus on *pedagogy*. Pedagogy is more than teachers and teaching, of course, but they are crucial to it nonetheless. Boomer led the way into reconsidering pedagogy, especially in the Australian context, bearing in mind that post-Dartmouth English teaching involves a different kind of teacher, as we have seen, and a new understanding of teaching. Hence he was concerned on the one hand with its codification, its documentation, which would provide better for what he called, provocatively, a 'science' of pedagogy and of English teaching, and on the other, he was constantly searching for better ways of developing and demonstrating it *in* practice and *as* practice, in what might be called a *vernacular* pedagogy – how it played out in and through practice. Practice and pedagogy, then: Boomer was undoubtedly a leading figure in moving the field on, and in opening up its future.

Notes

1. Moreover, Britton described this as "the age of the *classroom* teacher" (p. 11).
2. For example, in a 1982 manuscript entitled "In Search of Power: An Australian English Teacher in America", he noted that "[i]t is not by accident that I am currently preoccupied with questions of teacher power. Clearly in South Australia at the present time there are many looming pressures and new structures which pose a threat to *the power of teachers to act*" (my added emphasis) – something happening elsewhere as well, in and beyond this period (cf. Mayher, 1990).
3. See McKnight (2021) for a contemporary account of the durability of normative practices and perspectives, in this case with reference to writing pedagogy.
4. These are perhaps Stenhouse's notion of "extended professionals". He writes: "[T]he outstanding characteristics of the extended professional is a capacity for autonomous professional self-development through systematic self-study, through the study of the work of other teachers[,] and through the testing of ideas by classroom research procedures" (Stenhouse, 1975, p. 144). Boomer explicitly refers to Stenhouse in his essay "The English Teacher, Research and Change" (1988j [orig. 1982c]).
5. It was subsequently re-published in the AATE journal *English in Australia* and later in *Metaphors and Meanings* (Green, 1988) and it is the latter that is referenced henceforth.
6. See Mayher (2013) for an account of its reception in America. As he wrote, it was "very well received" at the 1984 NCTE Detroit convention, partly because of its rich vision of English teaching and partly because "[i]t was also a powerful counter-statement to the prevailing wind in American educational policy which was responding to a perceived crisis by investing even more heavily in standardised curricula and tests" (p. 22).
7. Note Boomer's own reference to educational journalism such as that of Kidder (1989), and perhaps also Rose (1989); for a more recent example, see Hicks (2014). That his account was drawn from original research is indicated in another of his papers of the time: "My recent research has required micro-analysis of one teacher and one class over

an extended period" (Boomer, 1988e, p. 183). This particular paper ("Reading Against the Grain") should be read therefore as a more hard-edged complement to the better-known 'Mrs Bell' essay.
8 This line is in fact taken from the 1985 version of the paper (Boomer, 1985g, p. 118) – subsequently re-published as Boomer, 1988h), which in fact ended slightly differently, with the added line "I challenge us all to continue to learn as much as possible about the loom and to weave with imagination".
9 This is published in the original 'Negotiation' volume (1982). See the Appendix, this volume.
10 There is a case to be made, I submit, that this title might have been itself edited, and rendered more appropriately as "Literacy: The Epic Challenge – Beyond Progressivism", This is a small matter perhaps, but defensible, I think, in the light of the discussion or 'reading' that follows. A good example, too, of the need for careful editing of Boomer's writing, which was often produced on the run, so to speak, and with therefore little time for working on nuances of expression or even argument. Elsewhere for instance he refers to "going through and *beyond* 'progressivism'" (Boomer, 1999g, p. 135), and this is what I see him as gesturing towards in the 'Epic' paper.
11 As he added: "That may be the case with many teachers too" (Boomer, 1988d, p. 154).
12 It emerges in several of the papers included in *Metaphors and Meanings* (Green, 1988), though perhaps it is named most firmly and clearly in "Negotiation Revisited" (pp. 168–178).
13 A point of disclosure here: I am identified in the text (p. 91) as having introduced Boomer to the Benjamin book, and this was indeed something we had previously discussed, on various occasions.
14 "Naturalistic theatre or film or performance is enactment which enthrals or captivates the audience by being so 'true to life' that there is willing suspension of disbelief. It is the art that conceals art. It works by surprising us – teasing us, wooing us – and takes pains to hide its origins and its intentions. In a very direct sense, naturalistic theatre is *charming*" (Boomer, 1999g, p. 91).
15 In making this point, I am mindful of Bernstein's work on 'visible' and 'invisible' pedagogies (1977), noting that this operated on the basis of a binary structure, thus marking that work as both structuralist and modernist in character (cf. similar formulations such as the notion of 'restricted' and 'elaborated' codes).
16 It should be said too that Boomer's original Darwin presentation was expressly performative, something some of his subsequent critics have missed, working as they must with simply the text. As Corcoran, 1998, p. 105) noted, ten years on: "what was missing from the printed page was 'Boomer's own epic performance where his revolutionary cap – a real one – was donned and discarded in self-conscious parody of the genre of a plenary address'". As Boomer (1999a, p. 95; my added emphasis) put it himself: "I rendered my [presented] text problematic by inventing an alter ego who argued with me on the podium. *I was trying to display publicly my private struggle to come to terms with a growing disquiet with some of the complacency and misguided practice which I saw as infecting the Language Arts scene*".
17 The original publication wasn't subtitled – although several chapters in that book (1982) were clear about the value of teachers operating as researchers in their own classrooms (see also Comber, 2013).
18 This was explicitly taken up in Green (1990a). Teachers' programming was explicitly linked with action research, on the one hand, and writing pedagogy, on the other. Programming – curriculum planning, or curriculum design – was described as a distinctive form of professional writing, and directly related to teachers' agency and organic professionalism.
19 Intriguingly, especially retrospectively, it wasn't included in the 1981 *Action Research Reader*, a central resource for the Australian action research movement that flourished in the 1980s (Kemmis, 1981). This is presumably notwithstanding that Boomer's paper

was originally presented at a Deakin symposium on action research earlier that year. Was this a missed opportunity? Or is it simply symptomatic of the familiar lack of recognition for work of this kind in the Academy? It should be acknowledged, nonetheless, that Boomer had various ties with Deakin over the years.
20 For work drawing on practice theory and philosophy, see Green (2009) and Kemmis and Mahon (2017); for a recent exploration of curriculum inquiry from such a perspective, see Green (2022).

4 Teaching English? Construing and (De)constructing the Territory

What marks out the territory of English teaching? What is it that makes subject English what it is, and distinctive and different as a curriculum formation? What do English teachers do that makes them *English* teachers? What marks them out? What *is* English? These are questions often asked since Dartmouth, and they are appropriately mobilised once more here, in seeking to lay out how Garth Boomer understood the field and the profession in the context of his time. He was acutely aware of the changed and changing nature of English teaching and the language arts in education, and deeply implicated and indeed a significant figure in effecting and encouraging such change. He was also always reflexive in himself, and with regard to his own work, and actively promoted reflexivity in both the field and the profession. Subject English itself was therefore properly questioned, as he saw it. He abhorred what he saw as 'mindlessness', especially professionally, or simply going with the flow – "Only dead fish swim with the stream", as he observed more than once (Boomer, 1988g, p. 179). So Boomer was interested in this question of territory, and moreover in territory as metaphor, which for him was a way of thinking about representation, although he didn't use that notion. 'Maps' and 'territories': these was constant themes throughout his work. What then can all this tell us about his view of subject English, and of what English teachers were to teach in the post-Dartmouth era?

What *Is* 'English'?

A notable feature of English teaching post-Dartmouth is its turn towards *activity*, albeit more commonly realised as 'process', and somewhat misleadingly so. In shifting to focus on 'reading' and 'writing', 'talking' and 'listening' (and, later, 'viewing' and 'making'), they were thus presented as verbs, rather than nouns, as traditionally and commonsensically. Boomer indeed made a similar point about 'curriculum', inviting us to think instead of 'curriculum-ing', in his characteristic way, and notwithstanding the fact that curriculum was the received term. A similar observation can be made for 'English', long a cornerstone of the Anglophone school curriculum. 'English-ing' clearly doesn't work. Yet the point remains that naming the subject as simply 'English' has proved problematical, in this instance because it evokes an entity and an identity and, in doing so, risks essentialism.

DOI: 10.4324/9781003374886-4

Something *had* changed in the post-Dartmouth era, however, and this is registered in various attempts right from the outset at describing the subject, none of which were all that successful. Dixon (1975) for example famously referred to English as the most 'quicksilver' of subjects, suggesting that grasping its character and identity was elusive, while Britton described English rather unfortunately as "the connective dough that was left after rolling out jam tarts and cutting them into circles" (Vee, 2020, p. 4).[1] This unwillingness – or inability – to present a coherent view of what subject English *is*, focusing rather on what it *does*, might be seen now as something of a fatal flaw, certainly from a curriculum-theoretical perspective, but also strategically, in that it weakened the subject's capacity to justify and defend itself, which has become increasingly necessary in more recent times.

Boomer was similarly reluctant to fully and clearly articulate how subject English was to be understood, in its specificity, relying perhaps on a sense that this was something received, or simply to be assumed – although doing so runs counter to his practice otherwise. He increasingly worked outside English teaching, moreover, consistent with his professional concerns with language and learning across the school curriculum, although remaining committed and connected to English teaching in various ways. Hence he wrote about literature and literacy, reading and writing, as well as drama and (to some extent) media, while in particular exploring the new possibilities associated with language as a crucial resource for learning. The former were established concerns, as it were, part of what Medway (1984) described as the norm for English, that is described elsewhere (Green & Beavis, 1996, p. 8) as "classroom activity organised around literature, writing, and 'language work'" (aka 'grammar'). In what follows, then, the focus will be firstly on Boomer's reflections on and arguments about literature and the turn to textuality and cultural studies, and secondly on his view of literacy and writing. In doing so, the aim is to explore his attitude to 'content' – the *what* of English teaching. As he asserted, 'content' matters: "[a] unit of work without solid content will be 'at risk'" (Boomer, 1992c, p. 36). That applied to subject English as much as anywhere else in the curriculum, although specifying just what that 'content' consists of in English has proved to be contentious. It will be assumed here that Boomer's view of language and learning more generally was consistent with those associated with, in particular, what has been called the London tradition, which means that he had a certain view of the English classroom and its characteristic organisation, marked by small group-work and active, collaborative learning, and a congruent and distinctive pedagogy.[2] Such classrooms featured, as a rule, much exploratory and reflective talk and writing, and an opening up of exchange between teachers and students. Doubtless he also shared much of that tradition's view of what English was concerned with, post-Dartmouth – a commitment, that is, to student voice and experience, as primary subject matter. Beyond that, of course, was the world itself, and being and becoming in the world, and making a difference in it.

Above all else, Boomer was pragmatic. He was always wary of bandwagons and doctrinal groups ('camps'). This can be seen early on in the way he operated regarding an intense 'language/literature debate' in the 1970s, over which category had priority as an organising principle for English. Stemming from Dartmouth, and signalling the new ascendancy of language and learning associated primarily with the so-called London School, this was always a misleading issue, at best. Boomer's own positioning here is evident perhaps most clearly in an essay he published in 1974 ("Eternal Triangles: Language and Literature in Senior English"), soon after his return from his London studies, and a fuller discussion is undertaken below. A similarly unproductive debate centred on a simplistic opposition which emerged in the 1980s, concerning the rival claims of 'process' and 'genre' in writing pedagogy. Boomer's view, exemplified most clearly in a 1985 essay ("Towards a Model of the Composing Process in Writing", 1985f), is instructive and illuminating, and this is also discussed more fully below. Perhaps the most striking indication of how Boomer sought to work across seemingly disparate positions, evident all too often in the historical record and the course of things, was his clear endorsement of Michael Halliday, notwithstanding his deep commitment to James Britton and his particular acknowledgement of Britton's influence. As he wrote (Boomer, 1988i, p. 29):

> It is a pity that many people see Halliday's view as opposed to that of Britton. Certainly Halliday reminds us, in contrast to Britton's emphasis on language as resource, of the importance of teaching about language, but his overarching metaphors are not sharply in conflict with Britton's.

Described early on as a major "map-maker" for the New English as it was emerging in Australia (Boomer, 1977, p. 10), Halliday remained throughout an important reference-point for Boomer, and for English teaching more generally. He represented the leading edge of what Boomer hailed as the new linguistics, "rescu[ing] language from the frozen chambers of post-mortem study" (Boomer, 1973, p. 76) and opening up the social world of language in use. But Boomer was first and foremost an educator, and an English teacher. While he recognised that linguistics was an important and even crucial factor in education, it wasn't sufficient as a disciplinary resource, since other fields were clearly relevant, including psychology, philosophy, and sociology, as well as literary and cultural studies. Ultimately the 1980s (and ongoing) debate might be seen, perhaps, as a struggle between the linguists and the educationalists, as distinctive (though related) perspectives – and Boomer, in the end, must clearly be identified with the latter. All the same, as we shall see, he always sought to see beyond such 'divides'.

In what follows, then, I firstly take up the question of 'literature' in Boomer's work, and his shift in this context to consider notions of 'text' and cultural studies. The following section is addressed to 'writing', and beyond that the chapter focuses on 'literacy'. The organising framework here is a conceptual framework which brings together *language, literacy,* and *literature* as interlinked historical concepts in English curriculum history (Green, 1990b, 2018c; Sawyer, 2013, p. 27).

English Teaching, 'Literature' and Cultural Studies

Whatever else it deals with, literature has remained central to English teaching, in one way or another. So it was for Boomer, it would seem – although, somewhat curiously, he did little formal writing on literature and its pedagogy in his body of work, as Sawyer (2013, p. 27) notes. Nonetheless he often used literary images and allusions in his presentations, and certainly he had a literary background. He was not entirely happy with what this entailed, however, if his early comments and observations are any guide. As he noted in 1973, "Perhaps when the academics have subjected some of their longstanding myths to scrutiny, literature will be taught, and justified, with more conviction as a dynamic and formative influence in society" (Boomer, 1973, p. 76). Drawing a distinction between literary studies as it was then and the new linguistics emerging at the time, he suggested that "at least in Australia, we wait for the gurus of literature to show the way to life", and until or unless they do, "whole legions of English teachers will continue to treat literature either with a kind of disengaged, ceremonial respect or else as documentary evidence to support their own social theories" (p. 76). This was the period before the impact of literary theory and cultural studies, which were just starting to break in Australia in the mid-1970s, and various shifts in the hierarchical relationship between universities and schools. Boomer had undoubtedly seen signs of these momentous developments in literary and cultural studies in his London sojourn, coming in contact as he did with the work of figures such as Raymond Williams and Roland Barthes, and others. As he wrote some years later, "just as a clearer conception of language is emerging, so there is an emerging new picture of literature as a fundamental human activity" (Boomer, 1988i, p. 28).

Soon after returning to Australia, he published one of the very few papers he did specifically on literature, under the title "Eternal Triangles: Language as Literature in Senior English" (Boomer, 1974/2010). A decade later, in 1984, he prepared a discussion paper entitled "Literature and English Teaching: Opening Up the Territory" (Boomer, 1988j)[3] for the IFTE Seminar held at Michigan State University in 1984, and a year later, followed it up with a summary statement ("Language, Literature and Human Values") of the deliberations of a study group which he convened at that seminar (Boomer, 1985d). What follows will be principally in reference to these texts; due acknowledgement is made here of Sawyer's (2013) account, which offers a particularly rich perspective on them and the prevailing context.

The decade in question here – that is, the period between the mid-1970s and the mid-1980s – is arguably when Boomer was most focused on (re)thinking English teaching *per se*. He subsequently shifted to more systemic and general concerns as he moved up and through the educational bureaucracy, taking on more managerial responsibility and various organisational leadership roles. He retained, however, a keen interest in English teaching and literacy education, in 1989 delivering a ground-breaking keynote address at the annual AATE conference held in Darwin (Boomer, 1999g) and presenting at various conferences overseas, notably in the United States (Boomer, 1993). The period is also extremely important, however, in terms of some of the most momentous changes in the field, embracing literary education, writing pedagogy, and language study. The focus in this section is on the former – on 'literature'.

On 'Literature' and Literary Study

Boomer's "Eternal Triangles" essay was a powerful early statement of a new wave in work on literary education and its place in English teaching, although curiously the essay itself seemed to attract little attention and is rarely cited. University English was experiencing rumbles of discontent, heightened with the mid-70s establishment of new universities in Western Australia and Queensland (Deakin and Griffith respectively), both of which encouraged innovative lines of scholarship and became key sites in the emergence of cultural studies (Frow, 2007) An important event more specifically in the context of school education was the Literature Commission in the 1980 IFTE conference, held in Sydney (Mallick et al., 1982). The Commission brought together "over 150 delegates from eight different countries – England, the United States of America, Canada, South Africa, India, China, New Zealand, [and] Australia" (p. 1). The conversations and debates were wide-ranging, as might be expected, and perhaps understandably inconclusive, although clearly there was an emergent focus on 'response' as an organising principle, something which became more insistent in the subsequent course of the decade.[4] There was little sign of the new literary theory, however, or indeed of cultural studies, with its more critical, sociological perspectives and interests, and its explicit engagement with media and popular culture.[5] This emerged later, in the important work of Ian Reid (1984), one of the first literary academics, certainly in Australia, to bring together university and school 'English', and moreover in a mutual exchange.[6] Sawyer (2013) has provided a succinct overview of other generative work in this period, taking up reader-response and reception aesthetics in literary studies[7] and, later, work more influenced by various versions of poststructuralism.

Boomer's early work in this regard is strikingly prescient, if a somewhat uneasy assemblage of disparate arguments and influences. The "Eternal Triangles" essay seeks to bring together the three-way relationship of *writer, text,* and *reader* with that of *teacher, text,* and *student*. The common point is the 'text', here understood simply as the literary work, or the object of study; thus, in the second instance, it effectively stands in for the curriculum, as in his later formulation regarding what he called "the eternal triangle of education" (Boomer, 1992a, p. 4). Boomer identifies, in fact, nine distinct but clearly related triangles, not altogether successfully, but the important thing is firstly the interplay of the above sets and secondly that together they form a network or field of interrelations. This 'network' is intriguing. It is predicated on two key assertions: (1) that "[t]he literary act is a complex social process", and (2) that "[t]he act of teaching literature further complicates the process" (Boomer, 1974/2010). Boomer then goes on to work through what he calls "the artist", "the work", and "the reader", respectively, as three organising nodes of this particular 'triangle'. Literature is presented as "the literary act", and hence as a social activity, first and foremost:

> By the literary act I mean the total chain of events which begins with a writer's experience, proceeds through his [*sic*] talking to himself, continues through composition to the birth of some kind of literature and then moves into the realm of contemplation and reception of the literary work by a reader; an act in which the writer converses indirectly with his reader.
>
> (Boomer, 1974/2010, p. 36)

The reader is similarly enmeshed in a social world. The emphasis is on process and relation, particularly the "various relationships involved in the composing and reading process" (p. 36). Writing and reading are thus brought together in literary activity, thus conceived.

For Boomer, literature is "language used in a social act", and accordingly "thorough teaching of literature should be based on a deep theoretical understanding of the nature of language and a fairly intensive examination of the sociology of literature" (p. 36). Literature is a particular form of language in use, that is, and understanding that particularity becomes important – what kind of language-in-use? What marks it out? What makes it so? Although his response to such questions isn't altogether satisfactory here, he does point to institutional considerations, including the selective nature of tradition and the significance of context(s), as well as stressing the play of intertextuality, not just with regard to literature itself but also to reading and pedagogy. Importantly he acknowledges the link between mature literary practice and that of children and young people, as well as in everyday life. This reminds us of Boomer's awareness of and affinity with the emerging debates associated with New English figures such as Britton and Rosen, and also Meek, in which no doubt he had recently immersed himself. Hence he writes, for example: "it seems to me that from the moment we start speaking with meaning around the age of two years, we are all continually striving at times to shape language into forms which are akin to literature" (p. 39). Crucially he points to the significance of 'contexts':

> As we have seen the writer in a matrix of contexts, so we can also view the work itself within the context of all past works; that is, within the context of institutionalised literature, within the context of the history of language and language associations and within the context of contemporary works.
>
> (p. 39)

Similarly with the reader ("the reader, too, has his [*sic*] own unique contexts – the context of past experience in both life and literature, the contexts of class and culture, of current fashions in aesthetics, and even the present situation"; p. 40), and with reading – marking thereby an emerging semiotic awareness, which he subsequently articulated much more explicitly.

A decade later, Boomer convened one of the five Study Groups ('Language, Literature, and Human Values') at IFTE's Michigan State gathering (Tchudi, 1985), for which he provided a pre-conference discussion paper ("Exploring the Territory and Raising Some Questions"). The report on the Study Group's deliberations was published subsequently (Boomer, 1985d), and presumably Boomer put it together. Other notable participants included Deanne Bogdan, Louise Rosenblatt, and Patrick Dias. Boomer was more assured by then in his sense of the new role and significance of 'literature', pointing indeed to a "possible reconceptualization of English teaching and literature education" (Boomer, 1988j, p. 100). The discussion paper demonstrates an increasingly informed *social* perspective, shading into a socially critical, socially transformative view. Boomer brings in ideology as well as pedagogy. As he writes, "literature is, indeed, produced and consumed. It is not magically given. It is not natural. It is socially constructed within socially shared conventions" (Boomer, 1988j, p. 100). Literature itself must now be seen as an expanded category, ranging from print to the audio-visual, and embracing the oral and the enactive: "I want schools to be places where children study the fullest range of literature, from oral-story-telling, to street theatre, to popular novels, to films and video plays" (pp. 101–102). This continues in the report. "Literature is any text, verbal and/or visual, that offers the possibility for aesthetic reading or viewing and listening" (Boomer, 1985d, p. 169).

Moreover, and importantly: "The goal of literature teaching is the enfranchisement and empowerment of children as learners and actors in the making of culture" (p. 170). There is now an explicit concern with empowerment, although pleasure and engagement remain extremely important. Emphasis is placed on *both* experience and analysis, with pedagogy attuned to 'first encounters' and 'close encounters' (Green, 2023), and once again we can see a developmental poetics being at once confirmed and adumbrated. This is congruent with but also directly informed by contemporaneous work by figures such as Ian Reid, referred to above, along with Louise Rosenblatt, Margaret Meek, and others. Once again there is an emphasis on critiquing and going beyond 'response':

> Unexplored, the word 'response' may too readily suggest reaction to a text almost on a stimulus-response model. This tends to distract us from a full appreciation of how literature is socially and ideologically constructed in the first place and then re-made in the act of reading.
> (Boomer, 1985b, p. 174)

Teaching needs to accommodate this, and yet ensure that "the place of student intentions in reading and writing" (p. 163) is properly and fully accounted for, within what is clearly a negotiation framework: "How can we bring about a communion between teacher and student so that literature can work for both?" (p. 163) – the links between communication and conversation, and curriculum, are clear. Emphasis is placed on connecting literacy and literature:

> The separation of literacy and literature seems to be a key concern[,] as is the efferent model of reading and writing most literary instruction is based on. It seems we need to redefine literacy in such a way as to link it more with literature.
> (Boomer, 1985b, p. 165[8])

New Directions

What is perhaps especially striking about Boomer's work here is his probing into new, and possibly even different, territory. He begins to ask questions about English itself, in exploring what has historically constituted its central 'content': "If we push out the boundaries of English teaching to include a wider range of literature, will English finally disappear as a subject?" (Boomer, 1988j, p. 102). This is to unsettle traditional associations of subject English with canonicity and heritage, and with particular notions of evaluation and discrimination. He explicitly noted the emergence of cultural studies, as increasingly both a reference-point and a resource for English teaching – in Australia, certainly, a growing factor in university English studies. This pertains not just to new study objects – 'texts', embracing a range of media, including print – but also new approaches and perspectives, such as critique and cultural criticism. He was increasingly oriented to the future, then – to the emergent. As he writes:

> I have been more and more teased in writing about the future of English teaching in this paper. I suspect we are moving to a new era when the term 'English' will have to go. My view is that the umbrella 'cultural studies' may more properly represent what we are offering to the curriculum. We are indeed about reading and making the world through reading and making literature, broadly defined. Aren't we?
>
> (Boomer, 1988j, p. 107)

This was a theme he later takes up explicitly in the introduction ("Dancing Lessons") to his selected essays on English teaching, where he acknowledges certain "patent insularities" in some of his early thinking, including a "tendency towards English-centeredness and a somewhat obsessive learning lens bias" (Boomer, 1988b, p. 7). His perspective and his purview had widened. His more recent work, as he indicates, had led him to "contemplate how the scope and purpose of English teaching might change as it becomes oriented to the consideration and possible solution of *cultural* problems through the reading and making of texts" (Boomer, 1988b, p. 7). He refers here to 'cultural literacy', a term he mobilised elsewhere, not in the then contemporaneous sense of E.D. Hirsch, but with a more critical inflection, akin to what subsequently is called, somewhat programmatically, 'critical literacy'. Working on 'cultural problems' is akin to what Peter Medway (1990b) associated with 'worldliness'.[9] Such a perspective opens up, but also complicates, the field, challenging it.

It is indeed worth citing him at length in this regard, and at this point. "It is pleasing", he writes, three years after the IFTE seminar, "to see how English teachers are beginning to liberate themselves from a narrow conception of the literary text", continuing thus:

> Once 'text' is conceived of as a cultural artefact, any text past, present or future, classic or popular, fiction or non-fiction, written, oral or filmic, can be

admitted to the English classroom for legitimate and rewarding scrutiny, from the standpoint of 'Who made this? In what context? With what values? In whose interests? To what effect?'

(Boomer, 1988b, p. 7)

This is essentially a (new) rhetorical stance, an acknowledgement of textual power (Green, 2006; Scholes, 1985). It has important implications for the subject and for the profession. "I see English teaching throwing off its long entrenched associations with a bookish capital 'C' culture", Boomer (1988b, p. 7) writes: "The new English will take its place in the total curriculum as a vigorous, hard-headed, socially-critical, productive field of engagement with the here-and-now through its work with texts" (pp. 7–8). The emphasis is thus clearly and firmly on *action*, or what might properly and appropriately be called praxis. As he concludes: "This might not constitute a paradigm shift in itself, but it will mean substantial change to the content and direction of English teaching" (p. 8). Indeed.

In summary: Boomer provided an important marker of changing emphases and emerging forces in literary study and English teaching in the important cusp period from the mid-1970s to the mid-1980s. By then his focus had shifted to more systemic concerns. But he was undoubtedly very aware of what was happening, in literary theory and cultural politics, and moreover played a significant role himself in making such developments central to English curriculum renewal.

Writing Pedagogy and the Literacy Debate

The 1980 IFTE conference held in Sydney has been described as a watershed moment in post-Dartmouth English teaching and "the high point of 'progressivism' or the 'new' English in Australia" (Kostogriz & Doecke, 2008, p. 259). Boomer was a keynote speaker, befitting his status as perhaps the premier figure in Australian English teaching at the time.[10] Writing pedagogy figured heavily in the topics addressed at the conference, which was quite understandable given that the landmark publication *The Development of Writing Abilities 11–18* was released just five years previously (Britton et al., 1975). Other notable writing scholars at the conference included Donald Graves and James Moffett, both of whom were particularly influential in Australia – Moffett perhaps more retrospectively, on reflection (Green & Sawyer, 2023). In the subsequent decade, two key debates emerged: one was a new emphasis on literacy in the media and elsewhere, and increasingly in policy, and the other was an intense and sometimes heated struggle between exponents of 'process' and 'genre' perspectives in writing pedagogy. Boomer was directly involved in the first debate, continuing a line of concern evident in his earlier work (Boomer & Spender, 1976). He wasn't as directly or actively engaged in the latter, the 'process/genre' debate, but it is likely that this was a strategic move on his part, as much as anything else, given what emerged as that debate's somewhat doctrinal character and his aversion to 'camps'. However, he was keenly interested in school writing and writing pedagogy, and this was a focus for some of his own work. This section concentrates mainly on one of his most interesting papers in this regard – "Towards a Model of the Composing Process", published in 1985 but written some time earlier, around the time of the Sydney IFTE conference.

It is worth making some brief comments first on another essay, entitled "Becoming the Reader Over One's Own Shoulder" (Boomer, 1985e). The reason for this is because the essay demonstrates two features of Boomer's overall project. One is his deep immersion in the London tradition, elsewhere identified as 'English-as-Language'. Language and learning as an organising principle is always the primary reference-point. The focus on speech (and speaking) is crucial here, as a foundation for language development. Among the influences noted are L.S. Vygotsky, G.H. Mead, George Gusdorf, and Michael Polanyi – central figures, in fact, in Britton's *Language and Learning* (1970). Britton was certainly a major influence, then, but it is important to note that so too was Halliday. This should remind us that what might be called English teaching's own linguistic turn, from the 60s on – the turn to language – is best seen as embracing *both* Britton and Halliday, which is how 'English-as-Language' is most appropriately understood. Mead is however the main reference here, as the subtitle indicates: "An Experiment in the 'Conversation of Gestures'".

The essay recounts how Boomer worked with his son, almost eight, in the joint composition of a fictional narrative, a 'story'. A division of labour was enacted, with Simon as composer, the principal storyteller, and his father as scribe. The relationship however was profoundly pedagogic, in the sense that it involved a carefully negotiated dance between the two parties, in terms of ownership, authority, responsibility, and meaning. The point was to demonstrate how the two worked together, in bringing about *writer* development and what might be called *writing* development – the production of a distinctive (written) text. It was made clear that Simon's composing capability was in advance of his writing skills, but also that this was to be seen as at once quite understandable and a proficiency, a resource, and certainly not something to be concerned about, a deficit, at this stage at least. The point, rather, was to focus on where he, as learner-writer, was going and what he was becoming – that is, as *becoming-writer*. Part of this involves understanding how speech and writing work together and how and where they differ. There is also the matter of becoming reflexive, as well as knowledgeable – and this is where the notion of becoming, metaphorically, the reader looking over the writer's own shoulder, as s/he writes, becomes important. In this case, it was the father-figure, who was overseeing the process of performing and inscribing the writing, as it emerged and was enacted – and who presumably would eventually become internalised, as a reader-figure: engaged, accepting, tactful, questioning, etc. Mead was clearly relevant here, but so too was Vygotsky. The teacher role was very clear. "[T]he child internalizes what it is to be a writer through the social interaction with readers, writers, and writing" (Boomer, 1985e, p. 39). How might the classroom be best organised to allow for this to happen, as richly and fully as possible? Hence the significance of the classroom-as-workshop, for Boomer (1988e) as much as Reid (1984).[11] "[I]f Simon is to become a writer, he must be exposed to the social process of communication through the written word and be encouraged to experiment with written 'gestures' (Boomer, 1985e, p. 40) – the classroom as writing workshop, with others (including the teacher) writing, reading, listening, performing...

Several strategies for storytelling were outlined, involving both the 'composer' and the 'scribe', with clear implications for both teaching and learning. In the former case, those provided were 'finding a way in' ("The first sentence of any writing is very important for the composer" – p. 41), "controlling the poetics and aesthetics of composing", "providing collaborative detail", "engineering",[12] "selecting language appropriate to the scenario", "prefiguring", "conducting inner dialogue", "sentence building", and "editing". Ten composing strategies, in this instance – Boomer often worked in this way, as it happens, drawing out what might otherwise be described as working principles. Similarly with the scribal function: "My task was to reflect back to him, as richly as I could, the effect he was having not just on me as his father, but also on the highly developed 'generalized other' within me" (Boomer, 1985c, p. 45). This entailed a number of distinct 'responsive' roles: the generalised other, the restrained editor, the aesthetic reader, the puzzled reader, the gourmet reader, the indwelling reader, the anticipating reader, the 'action replay' reader, the generous reader, the collaborator. The overall effect is striking. As Boomer (1985e, p. 50) wrote: "The strategies of storyteller and scribe provide some useful clues about ways of improving the teaching of composition". The essay remains a rich resource for writing pedagogy.

Boomer's interest was always in 'composing', which he saw as meaning making and mobilised often, as metaphor, for instance in relation to curriculum, as already noted. This focus is evident also in "Towards a Model of the Composing Process" (Boomer, 1985f), a paper which emerged out of a series of meetings in the late 1970s between a South Australian group interested in writing and another from Victoria, focused on narrative. Organised under the auspices of the national Language and Learning Project, Boomer was an active participant and thoroughly caught up in what he described as a period of "intense intellectual inspiration" (p. 131). His interest in this paper was in how writing-as-composing was understood, or 'modelled'. How did writing pedagogy *think* about the practice of writing, and what was changing in that regard, in the context of new professional knowledge? How might it best be synthesised? This was in a period in which, as he writes, "the work of James Britton, James Moffett and Michael Halliday had considerable impact on the contents and spirit of official departmental curriculum guides" (p. 132) across Australia, although how much that was being picked up at the classroom level, in practice, was unclear and uncertain. Boomer's concern here, as elsewhere, was to articulate what was all too often largely tacit, and make it more explicit, and hence available for deliberation and interrogation. Ever mindful of what he called the "feverish alliances" associated with new ideas, he was seeking a personal synthesis of the major models prevailing in writing theory and pedagogy, with a view to "moving towards a more complex understanding of the whole composing process in the belief that unless we teachers find a comprehensive theory of the process, the teaching of writing will be subject to potentially toxic localized tinkering and transplanting" (p. 133). His focus on teachers – their needs, their knowledge – is notable, once again. And, as always, his aim was to move "towards a model, or models, of the composing process" (p. 133), rather than offering up a single definitive statement, a 'truth'.

Hence the paper brought together various formulations of what he calls "the writer's composing behaviours", which were seen as varying according to "the kinds of constraints and influences bearing on the *social* act of writing" (p. 133; my added emphasis). Reference was made in this context to "identifiable common *stages*, recursive not linear" in writing, with these stages described moreover as "essential". In this regard, the view endorsed was the then familiar process-developmental model associated with recent work by scholars working in the USA and the UK, and highly influential in Australia and elsewhere. "The 'composing process'" is presented as

> the *process* by which a writer *sequences* a set of *composing behaviours* in a certain *style* in order to make a piece of writing. It embraces all *stages* from the taking up of an intention to write through to the completion of the writing act.
> (pp. 133–134)

The paper goes on to review a range of accounts, bringing together a good sample of then contemporary and leading-edge writing scholarship. This is summarised as three (more or less recursive) 'stages', namely 'prewriting', 'writing' and 'postwriting'. That particular formulation is, in itself, unexceptional. It is subject, certainly, to the kinds of criticism made since by Joe Harris (2012) and others regarding 'process' perspectives in composition and writing pedagogy. The important point here however is that Boomer is concerned above all else with what this means, and yields, for teachers and teaching. Rather than the impoverished one-off scenario with which the paper opens – teacher assigns writing, perhaps with some preceding or accompanying stimulus activity, student writes, teacher marks (literally!) – each of the 'stages' identified can be seen as a *space for teaching* (indeed, for pedagogy), room and also opportunity for the teacher to work with the student(s), towards something that matters. The view of writing pedagogy that emerges is indeed rich and generative.

But even more interesting and important was Boomer's movement beyond what was described as the "two-dimensional analysis of function and audience" (p. 135) commonly associated with Britton and Moffett, the significance and influence of which he fully acknowledged. As he wrote:

> While accepting the powerful effect of audience and function, the Victorian-South Australian group (Kress et al.) ... concluded, after examining samples of children's writing, that form or genre had been a major influence on the composing behaviour of the writer, especially on semantic and lexico-syntactic options which had been taken up.
> (p. 135)

That is, there were "three significant tensions" shaping and animating writing, which he identified in terms of the following questions: "What is my purpose?

Who is my audience? What form shall I use and how conventional shall I be?" (p. 136). Function, audience *and* genre: a three-dimensional model. Boomer's elaboration of what this entailed remains instructive, notwithstanding the advances made since in the field. There can be no doubt that he recognised, and acknowledged, the specific role of language in writing and the value of linguistics in this regard: he makes insightful use of Halliday's notion of 'meaning-potential' and other key terms, including the 'macro-functions'. But what remains intriguing, certainly from a curriculum-historical point of view, is how this argument was entirely overlooked in what followed, in the 1980s and beyond.

The paper itself was little cited, if at all. Instead, the period saw a fierce and sometimes heated debate conducted between proponents of what became known as 'process' and 'genre' pedagogy, respectively. This was first neatly summarised in Reid's edited monograph *The Place of Genre in Learning: Current Debates* (1987), and it has re-emerged a number of times, in different forums, subsequently. It remains current today, in the turn to writing in education policy, in Australia, which seems to be predicated on the apparent success of genre pedagogy and the eclipse of its other, the process-developmental perspective long associated with English teaching, and indeed of English teaching itself, in this particular policy turn. What Boomer offered was a way of integrating, or at least bringing into dialogue, two otherwise contending lines of argument and analysis: an integrated view that allowed for considerations of function, audience *and* genre to be explored, in their implication for and effect on writing pedagogy.[13] The opportunity was certainly there. Even if Britton's particular functional model was open to question, others such as Douglas Barnes (e.g., Barnes & Barnes, 1983, 1986) were calling for an extension of the range of rhetorical functions. Moffett's effective disappearance from the scene of writing pedagogy has been noted elsewhere (Green & Sawyer, 2023), and not just in Australia, notwithstanding the case to be made for his continuing significance and value.

The debate continues.[14] While it is neither appropriate nor possible to go into details here, one explanation worth considering is that the struggle has been of a disciplinary nature, between the 'educationists', on the one hand, and the 'linguists' on the other. That is, it has involved a particular realisation of the politics of disciplinarity. While Boomer was undoubtedly open to the contribution and involvement of linguistics,[15] he was nonetheless an educator first and foremost, a teacher, and oriented accordingly to work in an interdisciplinary way in matters concerning language learning and development, and curriculum and schooling more generally. His affinity in this regard with Britton is marked. Nancy Martin (1988, p. xiii) has observed that "education, of which English is a part, is compounded of many disciplines", pointing to Britton's characteristically interdisciplinary (and even pre-disciplinary) perspective, itself predicated to some extent on his sense of practitioners' pragmatism – "Teachers are pragmatists in a field drawing from many disciplines" (Britton, 1977, cited in Martin, 1988, p. xiv).[16] This was certainly Boomer's position as well: he constantly worked from what might be called the practitioner standpoint, and he was adamant about teaching as a form of pragmatic-radical professionalism, as we have seen.

Engaging the Literacy Debate

It remains simply to point to Boomer's role in what is commonly called the Literacy Debate, but which at various times modulates into the 'Standards Debate' or the 'Literacy Wars' (Snyder, 2008).[17] This is commonly seen as gathering momentum in the 1970s and fully breaking out in the following two decades, although it is better seen as a post-war phenomenon (Green et al., 1997) and as associated with the post-60s emergence and consolidation of the New Right. Boomer was quickly engaged over the course of the 70s, recognising that literacy was indeed a new player in the public discourse, with profound implications for schooling and teaching, and providing active leadership in this regard (e.g., Boomer, 1976). While he was not associated with the emergence of literacy studies as a new scholarly endeavour, he remained vigilant about the new focus on literacy in policy and the media, and certainly registered the controversy surrounding educational standards, increasingly featuring in public debate. Somewhat ironically but also quite understandably, he later took up this motif of 'standards' himself (Boomer, 1992e), in his senior educational-bureaucratic role, in advocating for national 'statements' and 'profiles', a precursor to national curriculum initiatives in the early 21st century. What is clear, however, is that he continued to work with practice and practitioners in mind, as a key reference-point: "As I read it, the profiles approach comes out of a strongly teacher-centred, classroom-oriented understanding of how judgement works on a day to day basis in our schools" (Boomer, 1992e, p. 64).[18]

Recognising literacy as a new organising principle, Boomer began to mobilise his own version of 'cultural literacy', as a potential rallying-point. Hence he argued for newspapers to be drawn critically into classroom work, with 'cultural literacy' understood as "reading and writing the world, figuratively speaking" (Boomer, 1987b, p. 52), within the context of "a school curriculum which is socially constructive and socially productive" (p. 55). It is highly likely he was aware of Hirsch's controversial but also influential book on 'cultural literacy' published around the same time (Hirsch, 1987), and if so, he would have seen this as an opportunity – at once rhetorical and (counter-)hegemonic – to intervene by seeking to appropriate the term and re-articulate it. The similarities, nonetheless, with the other formulation gathering momentum at this time – 'critical literacy' – are obvious. In his work on newspapers he introduced the notion of 'text' that we have seen elsewhere, as a *framing*: "By text I do not mean something written. By 'text' I mean anything written or enacted or experienced which is *framed* in some way that makes it amenable to analysis and comprehension". This is much akin to the views of textuality associated with figures such as Derrida or Ricoeur. In this particular sense, then, "all human experience is potential *text* which can help us towards greater cultural literacy" (Boomer, 1987b, p. 52). He later pointed to education and the media as "the major text-makers of [the] modern nation" (Boomer, 1999h, p. 71). Media, he suggested, constitutes its own form of curriculum. It was implicated in cultural formation – or rather, in "cultural confirmation and consolidation", and even "cultural colonisation" (p. 77). This applies as much to newspapers and magazines as to television and radio, as "text-makers". Hence, as he wrote: "In our schools, we need to teach for cultural literacy and thoughtful capability, so that the citizens of tomorrow will demand better media and still better schools" (p. 79). Newspapers, like media generally, were thus properly the province of English teaching, along with Media Studies, as both "crucial areas for the nurturing of questioning and demanding consumers of newspapers and television" (p. 79). In this respect Boomer can be seen as clearly working towards a reconceptualised, cultural-critical view of English-as-literacy, consistent with his arguments elsewhere for dialogue between English and cultural studies.

Conclusion

What to teach in English? What counts as English? What are the particular responsibilities and concerns of English teaching? What goes on in English classrooms? These have been the questions driving this chapter, pointing to the specificity of subject English. The distinction is all too often blurred, as we have seen, with 'English' understood as both the school-subject and the medium of curriculum and schooling. Boomer, like others central to the post-Dartmouth tradition, provided clear and decisive leadership in the latter regard, with his work on language and learning and language across the curriculum. But he was also actively concerned with English teaching *per se*, as a distinctive curriculum formation, and one he remained heavily invested in and identified with. Whatever else subject English has been concerned with, it has been literature and writing that have been constant features of English work, and teaching literature and writing arguably remains central to the subject-area, albeit in ways consistent with the new media ecology embracing both print and digital-electronics. Boomer provided important guidelines to where he thought English teaching was going, and history has largely proved him right.

At the same time he remained sceptical about the English curriculum as a received formation, linked more or less organically to heritage and canonicity. This applied as much to writing as to literature, as key and recurring components – all the more so when we recall that, for many, a pervasive literariness characterises much of the traditional writing curriculum. Further, as we have seen, Boomer sensed that somehow 'literature' was central to subject English's identity and hence extending the ambit of the literary – or perhaps, from another perspective, weakening it – challenged the very *raison d'etre* of English as a school-subject: "[W]ill English finally disappear as a subject?" (Boomer, 1988j, p. 102). In which case, what might be its successor-subjects? What all this did allow for was a sense of subject English as a cultural invention – having been constructed, it could be changed. It could be re-constructed, *and* de-constructed.

It is at this point that we can go back to earlier discussion of Boomer's growing awareness of text/context dynamics in curriculum and English teaching. As well as highlighting changing understandings of text, he increasingly drew attention to the significance of *context*. This can be extrapolated to suggest that text and context are themselves marked not only by multiplicity, at least potentially, but also interchangeability. So increasingly Boomer pointed to curriculum *as* text – "a web of textuality" (Pirie, 1997) – at the same time as he advocated for a curriculum *of* texts, as focused on and organised by textuality. This is why he began to work explicitly with a Brechtian perspective, in seeking to unsettle and estrange the curriculum, and to encourage what he called a healthy scepticism, a healthy "alienation effect". As he wrote, apropos the value and even the necessity of asking difficult questions about curriculum and schooling, teaching, and learning:

> When you start asking such questions of the school's curriculum, it is no longer possible to think of it as 'natural'. You have to become like the audience at a Brechtian play, a healthily alienated inquirer who knows that the curriculum is a performance generated within the school's culture, a demonstration that has palpable designs on you. It is no longer a *given*; it is a way of *taking*, now that you have learnt to act on it.
>
> (Boomer, 1988d, pp. 156–158)

This applies to subject English as much anything else. To ask questions about why this (this novel, this 'text') is being studied rather than that, or this other one, is to make the whole process and experience of curriculum problematic, and thus to denaturalise it. Sometimes the distinction between 'map' and 'territory' is itself blurred, and maybe the terms themselves can become interchangeable. Is this kind of inquiry what goes on in English lessons? Should it? There is pedagogic *and* social value in doing so, surely.

Notes

1 Britton offered this observation at Dartmouth, in responding to a paper entitled 'What is English?' by Albert Kitzhaber, who was presenting a distinctive American perspective on the matter. As Britton (1966) put it: "My mother used to make jam tarts and she used to roll out the pastry and I remember this very well – I can still feel what it is like to do it, although I have never done it since. She used to roll out the pastry and then she took a glass and cut out a jam tart, then cut out another jam tart. Well we have cut out geography, and we have cut out history, and we have cut out science. What do we cut out for English? I suggest we don't. I suggest that is what is left. That is the rest of it" (, p. 12, Section A1). English, that is, "is what's left" of the pastry, once all the other subjects are accounted for – hardly a satisfactory or reassuring view of subject English, it seems to me. At the time, however, it may well have been a liberating view, and I readily acknowledge that.
2 The latter is elaborated in Chapter 3.
3 Originally presented as "Exploring the Territory and Raising Some Questions", the paper was retitled in the 1988 collection of Boomer's essays on English teaching (Green, 1988).
4 Margaret Meek's contribution needs to be noted here. Her paper ("Response – Begin Again") sought to problematise 'response', as well as outlining what I think can appropriately be called a 'developmental poetics' (Meek, 1982; see Green, 2023).
5 Exceptions were the contributions of David Homer (1982) and Peter Moss (1982) – see also Homer (2003) for an account of largely South Australian work of the 1980s ('Category B'), which adopted an overtly critical stance on the field. Boomer was clearly influenced by such work, and published with them (Boomer, 1988g).

6 Reid was an active participant in the Sydney IFTE conference's Literature Commission (Reid, 1982).
7 An important Australian contribution at this time was Jack Thomson's study of literary education and teenagers' reading processes (Thomson, 1987).
8 Citing David Dillon, one of the participants in the Study Group.
9 More recently, there are intriguing links to be made in this respect with what has been described as "problems that matter" (Zipin, 2020), proposed as an 'activist' organising principle for curriculum work.
10 His Keynote Address was entitled "The English Teacher, Research and Change (1966–1980)", published originally in Eagleson (1982) and subsequently in Green (1988).
11 For Boomer's version of the classroom-as-workshop, see his essay "Teachers Learning" (1988e). Having evoked "[t]he ideal classroom for language development", he wrote: "Such a classroom, when knowledge about language has been translated into appropriate methodology, would be, at least: active and interactive, collaborative, functional and purposive, exploratory, reflective, multi-modal, negotiated, contextually supportive, observed and tracked, experience-based, text-aware, conceptually demanding, unbounded and cumulative" (p. 198). This 'ideal' still seems worth striving for.
12 An interesting term, picking up on the writer's ongoing maintenance and (project-) management of the text in formation, its 'architecture'.
13 See also Green (1987) for a similar argument. Boomer's initiative can be seen in retrospect as a response to a missing element in the original London writing study (Britton et al., 1975) – a focus on language itself, what they acknowledged as "the language resources that a child draws on in order to write" (p. 16). This element, potentially a 'third dimension', was presented as something still being developed at the time, and while 'genre' was explicitly noted, it wasn't seen then as either workable or appropriate, in that available formulation. Since it is very likely that Boomer knew the London work, he may well have come to recognise the salience of this point in his collaboration with Gunther Kress and others in the Narrative Working Party.
14 This must be further qualified by noting that, as of the 2020s, a recent shift in Australian education policy to focus on writing indicates that genre theory may have emerged as more successful in this regard, in some circles at least – suggesting further consolidation of the rise of standardised testing and assessment outlined in Reid's Introduction to Reid (1987). This matter is resumed in the concluding chapter.
15 "I am convinced that linguists have much to offer teachers, if, with a sensitive appreciation of the teacher's problems, they can develop appropriate ways of giving access to what they know" (Boomer, 1985f, p. 146).
16 Britton goes on thus: "[Teachers] have to be theorisers too, but their theorising stops at *a point nearer the phenomena* than does a linguist or psychologist whose theories have a bearing on education but are developed within other disciplines" (cited Martin, 1988, p. xiv; my added emphasis).
17 At issue in such 'debates' is always the question of 'grammar', and also relatedly, of 'phonics', and more recently 'direct instruction'. Boomer had little to say about language study *per se* in English teaching, although he would not have been sympathetic to explicit teaching of grammar, out of context. See the treatment of language in the textbooks he co-wrote with Christine Davis, *Reading and Writing 1* (1980) and *Reading and Writing 2* (1981), aimed at Years 1–2 in high school English.
18 Although this important (and controversial) aspect of Boomer's work is not developed here, it needs to be noted, nonetheless, as it pertains to his keen sense of the significance of assessment in curriculum and literacy, and also of the growing emphasis on accountability.

5 Conclusion
Neoliberal Conditions and Larrikin Lessons

That was then, this is now. How relevant is Garth Boomer today? What would he have contributed in today's educational environment? How can he be read today? Is his work and his thinking still relevant, in current neoliberal conditions? – a new order of things, educationally and socially. He died in 1993, just as the world was changing, inexorably, although it is now clear that this had been already underway over the previous decade. Thirty years later, how do we gauge his contribution to the field and the profession?

This concluding chapter will attempt to respond to such questions, on the way to affirming his continued importance as a key thinker in English education and the language arts and the ongoing relevance of his insights and arguments, his writing and his teaching. This is certainly the case for Australia, but also arguably for the wider international field, across the Anglophone educational world. The case will be made, in fact, that his particular perspective, his vision, his substantive thought, and his subversive energy is much needed, now as much as ever before, and re-visiting his work and looking at it in a renewed light at this time might well prove to be both inspirational and aspirational, and hence a resource for the future.

It needs to be recalled, too, that Boomer forged a distinctive path in the field, moving from a deep involvement and engagement with classrooms and teaching to the educational bureaucracy at the highest levels. His leadership in this latter regard is directly connected with his curriculum leadership, more specifically with the field of English teaching and literacy education. In many ways his influence and achievement extended beyond the particular field of English teaching and literacy education – he was described at one point as "perhaps Australia's most creative curriculum expert" (Collins, 1995, p. 13), for instance, and as "a crucial reference-point in late twentieth-century curriculum inquiry in Australia" (Green, 2003b; see also Green, 2021a). But there is no doubt that his base remained in English teaching and language-and-learning theory. It might even be argued that this in many ways resourced his work in other areas and arenas, for example in his essay on democracy in classrooms and the educational bureaucracy (Boomer, 1999d).

Questions of Compromise

As he wrote in a 'letter' to James Britton, from his vantage-point as then a senior bureaucrat, he had become much more realistic about constraints and compromise

DOI: 10.4324/9781003374886-5

than he had been ten years previously, in the late 1970s. He recognised that curriculum change was much more a matter of "negotiating the system", as a dynamic whole. Hence he pointed to

> how we are learning to work at all levels of the system at once, and how, at our best, we are abandoning labels in order to work with people of like mind, whose ideas have been generated in different ways, in different contexts, and are represented in slightly different language.
> (Boomer, 1988a, p. 240)

He continued thus:

> We are also coming to understand that, to enable teachers to apply the principles of language and learning, that you have advocated, we need to change the ruling discourse and the containing structures of society. This requires a sophisticated theory about systems and the way they work, as well as a learning theory.
> (p. 240)

Indeed, his experience of different roles as an educator and his distinctive trajectory into and within the bureaucracy positioned him well for this struggle, providing him with diverse lines of sight and angles of strategy. He recognised accordingly that politics was as important as pedagogy. This important insight was central to his curriculum leadership, in fact, in English and beyond, and he was fearless in exercising the right to critique, alongside a firm sense of possibility. As Barbara Comber (2013) correctly and aptly observed: "Boomer's critical insight and his preparedness to name and confront educational shortcomings as a leading educational bureaucrat was rare then, and some may argue even rarer today" (p. 55).

As already noted, this wasn't without cost. He found himself under heavy criticism at times from the mainstream field and even his own constituency – even close colleagues and friends – who were sometimes disappointed in his later 'career' moves or dismayed by his decisions. As one commentator, a peer, eloquently remembered:

> Garth told me once that one of the hardest things about rising up the seniority/promotion 'pole' of responsibility and accountability was that as you moved up into these higher 'atmospheres' you acquired – and had to cope with – a whole range of new knowledge, new contexts, new imperatives, and new responsibilities. This meant that decisions you would need to take informed by such new realities were seriously susceptible to criticism from your former colleagues whose very roles meant that they would not have been aware of such matters.
> (Brock, 2013, p. 15)

Charges were levelled at him, inevitably, of 'selling out', of becoming 'academic', of being seduced by 'power' and recruited into the 'system', the new corporate world-order. He was well aware of this. As he observed himself, in an interview: "one of the big stories that [is] being written [now] is that many of the senior educators in Australia, including the director-generals, would say that we've now got Boomer on-side" (Boomer, 1992d, p. 42). He was referring to his involvement in momentous shifts towards standardisation in education policy at the time (i.e., 1990), and the perception that this represented a recapitulation on his part, and for some at least a betrayal. As he continued:

> [Boomer]'s telling the story that we've been wanting, [that] we were wishing he would tell for a long time, he's been resisting, [but] he's now come across to us – so you know if someone like that has come across, in a way it indicates the sense of what we're on about. He's finally seen sense…
>
> (p. 42)

Although we must be careful here not to see informal statements such as these as 'truth', nonetheless they can serve as testimony, bearing in mind that it was indeed an increasingly difficult stage in his career and even his life. Elsewhere he refers to "the bleak winds of 1987" (Boomer, 1988a, p. 234), specifically compared to a decade earlier, with clear signs of major change in education and schooling. This surely applied as much in the UK as in Australia, and elsewhere – with national curriculum and assessment looming, in various forms and manifestations, and the emergence in social policy of what is being increasingly recognised as neoliberalism.

The Way Things Are – or, Neoliberalising English Teaching?

Alan Reid worked with Boomer and has written about him and the influence of his work (Reid, 2011, 2017). He has also written since of the 30 years or so of neoliberalism in Australian education (Reid, 2019). Describing neoliberalism as "the political and economic settlement that has dominated the western world for the past forty years, since the collapse of Keynesian economics and the welfare state in the early 1970s", he presents it as based on a belief that "in an unfettered free market, neoliberalism places the individual and 'individual responsibility' at its core, and so marginalises or rejects concepts such as the 'public good' and 'community'" (p. xx). It therefore constitutes a sharp contrast to the educational world Boomer was associated with, and, importantly, the historical legacy of public education. Reid points in particular to "the late 1980s onwards, when the shadow of neoliberalism fell upon [Australian] education" (p. 19), featuring an emphasis, discursively and ideologically, on a new logic of "markets, choice and competition" (p. 21). He describes among other things the rise of standardised testing, and standardisation more generally, as symptomatic, along with the exclusion of "the professional expertise of teachers from policy-making decisions" (pp. xv, Note 1) and the growing demoralisation and disaffection of teachers. Observing the resilience of neoliberalism, which he describes in 2019 as "still the dominant ideology in the western world", he writes:

> So entrenched is neoliberal philosophy that it appears to be a law of nature; so powerful are its ideas that they have shaped our language, and the way we see the world, ourselves and the alternatives that are open to us in the future.
> (p. 5)

He sees this "language and ideas" – its discourse – as having become "so embedded in public discourse that it seems as though they are natural laws, regardless of the contradictions and paradoxes they embody" (p. 13).

This is quintessentially Boomer territory, as indicated throughout this book: his profound insight into the problem of the 'natural', or rather, what has been 'naturalised' – becoming what might be called *second nature*. This 'second nature', or what is so taken for granted, is also something to question, to be suspicious about. As he insisted: "Curriculum is never 'natural', or inevitable". He cites Roland Barthes in this regard, slightly amended:

> We require an education in [curriculum] as in sentiments in order to discover that what we assumed – with the complicity of our teachers – was nature was in fact culture, that what was given was no more than a way of taking.
> (Boomer, 1988d, p. 154)

This play off between 'nature' and 'culture' is a feature, in fact, of Boomer's overall project. He was ever mindful of the dangers of reification, of formulations becoming formulas, ideas congealing into myths, of practices turning into institutions and staying fixed in place, evermore. In this regard, he was close in spirit to Marx, in his dialectical thinking and his suspicion of the surface appearance of reality, which is consistent with his interest in figures such as Brecht and Benjamin. This might be seen, in fact, as aligned with Boomer's concern with 'science' – for him, a critical perspective usefully and appropriately understood in terms of what has been called "a properly scientific stance" from a Marxist perspective.[1] And it is another aspect of Boomer's sometimes underestimated intellectual and political sophistication, or at least another possibility in terms of (re-)reading his work.

As it was, he was very clear about what was happening to education, and by extension, English teaching and literacy education. This included new regimes of testing and measurement, accountability and efficiency, regulation and control. Among these was an increasing – and for him, misguided – focus on scripted or prescribed pedagogy: "There is strong hegemonic pressure on systems, schools and teachers to revert to a direct-instruction, transmission mode of operation" (Boomer, 1988a, p. 238). This was something he was deeply concerned about, along with the consequent pressure on teachers and teaching, and their potential disaffection and even alienation. The resurgence and re-emphasis in Australia on 'direct instruction' or on 'phonics' in present-day liberal-conservative media – ostensibly directed towards improving outcomes for disadvantaged students – would have horrified him, although he is likely not to be all that surprised by their persistence and recycling. Given his own interest in writing pedagogy, too, he would have been struck by the most recent focus on writing in education policy, now in the spotlight again, after the previous focus more specifically on reading and various manifestations of the Literacy Debate. It is worth looking a little more closely at this particular development, then, in order to further reflect on Boomer's work and legacy.

Writing/Policy? – An In(ter)vention

We have already seen in Chapter 4 how the so-called 'process/genre' debate played out, particularly in Australia. He evoked the debate in various places, notably in the "Helping Hand" essay, but also in various other conference presentations towards the end, for instance at an Australian Reading Association national conference in 1991, where he is quoted as saying:

> I must say, that some of [the] material purporting to assist teachers in the teaching of aspects of genre carries with it many of the things I thought we'd learnt about what not to do in the teaching of grammar; that is, front-end loading it and teaching as prescription in a transmission mode.
>
> (Wildash, 2014, p. 12)

As he also observed, in what was in fact a familiar refrain: "Any regime, any method or non-method taken to extremes will be toxic" (p. 12). It is interesting to wonder, therefore, how he would have reacted to the new writing-focused policy initiative.[2]

First announced in a New South Wales newspaper article ("Teachers Fear They Lack Skills in Writing") in 2018, the unfolding narrative followed the well-documented script of the Literacy Debate (Green et al., 1997), albeit introducing a new object of concern – 'writing'. This concern refers at once to *students* (and their writing) and to *teachers* (and their teaching of writing), with both perceived as deficient, as 'lacking'. Writing is poorly taught in NSW schools, the article asserts. It reports a survey study of writing, later published under the title "Teaching Writing: Report of the Thematic Review of Writing" (NSW Education Standards Authority, 2018). The Report's principal writer had previously published a paper on 'NAPLAN' and writing pedagogy (Wyatt-Smith & Jackson, 2016). As the newspaper article notes, further: "Professor Claire Wyatt-Smith said classroom time should be set aside for students to practise writing and teachers to model it, as well as for 'a sustained focus on the teaching of grammar and linguistic features right through … schooling'" (Baker, 2020, p. 8). The formal Report itself was based on available data, notably that associated with the National Assessment Program – Literacy and Numeracy (NAPLAN), a compulsory standardised test applied across the board at Grades 3, 5, and 9. It is important to note that this program has been a matter of sustained critique and widespread criticism (e.g., Gannon, 2019). Reid (2019, p. 22*f*) specifically points to NAPLAN as exemplifying his account of standardised testing as a key aspect of neoliberalism in Australian education.

The policy turn to writing pedagogy has since been embraced across Australia more generally, coinciding with the emergence of a new body on the scene, the Australian Educational Research Organisation (AERO), established in 2020 to promote a more evidence-based approach to education policy and practice. AERO has since produced two reports, *Writing and Writing Instruction: An Overview of the Literature* (February 2022) and *Supporting Students Significantly Behind in Literacy and Numeracy: A Review of Evidence-Based Approaches* (May 2023). Both take a line on writing pedagogy consistent with that already outlined. A further study, from the conservative think-tank The Centre of Independent Studies, is entitled "Writing Matters: Reversing a Legacy of Policy Failure in Australian Education" (Clary & Mueller, 2021). The picture here is very clear. The history of writing pedagogy in Australia, in theory and practice, is presented as one of failure and neglect, a 'deficit' story. Effectively there has been nothing of note, and nothing to note.[3]

Clearly, the 'genre' camp has won the battle, officially at least. Moreover, English teaching has been eclipsed as both a resource for writing pedagogy and an authority on it. This is made very clear in the newspaper article mentioned above. There, calls for "responsibility for teaching writing to be given back to English teachers rather than sharing it across all disciplines" thereby cancel out the legacy of writing and literacy across-the-curriculum initiatives. One 'policy veteran' is cited as saying that "the chief responsibility for teaching writing should be returned to English teachers" (p. 1): "'When it was made everyone's business, it then became nobody's business', he said; 'Without English teachers being responsible for teaching writing as a foundation, no one is actually accountable'" (p. 8). This extraordinary statement is surely something that, as Boomer once observed,[4] you could "drive a few trucks through"…

How might Boomer have responded to NAPLAN? To the 'misguided' focus on writing practice and pedagogy in education policy? To the re-positioning of teachers as 'fearful' and lacking the necessary knowledge and skills, whose teaching is in 'deficit', and who are clearly in need of a "helping hand"? What can we learn from Boomer, even now?

One thing he would have encouraged, undoubtedly, is a clear-headed view of the big picture, of the larger context of educational and social change, and of what he called the "cosmic egg" of classrooms and teaching (Boomer, 1999a, p. 115) – the nest of contexts comprising the global 'force-field' of curriculum and schooling. He would have also cautioned against nostalgia, or dwelling in the past – perhaps in the spirit of Brecht's aphorism, 'Better the bad new days than the good old days'… But he would have insisted on respecting history, nonetheless, and the crucial value of learning from it. History was (and is) a resource, a necessary one, even if the future is something that must be properly reckoned into account, especially given new global anxieties about climate and security. We have also seen, above, where his own work, in the early 1980s, pointed to ways of thinking differently and more comprehensively about writing pedagogy (Boomer, 1985f). His thinking at that time cut across the binary nature of the 'process/genre' debate and "the wars of the language world" (Boomer, 1999f, p. 32) and offered new possibilities of dialogue and synthesis, at higher levels of articulation. This is akin to Luke and Freebody's classic intervention in the reading pedagogy field with their four 'resources' model, or even the 3D literacy framework (Green & Beavis, 2012), which brought together dominant discourses in literacy pedagogy. Rather than automatically thinking in 'either-or' terms, that is, we might look to what happens when a 'both-and' logic is brought to bear. It needs to be said, too, that Boomer's inclination was always to take an *educational* perspective as his baseline, focusing on learning, and teaching for learning, and this meant working in an interdisciplinary and even trans-disciplinary manner, rather than in strictly disciplinary terms. While he acknowledged the role and value of linguistics, there was always more at issue than the strictly linguistic, and for him educational thinking was enriched accordingly. Besides, he was sceptical about the pedagogy involved in academic-disciplinary transmission *per se*.[5]

Speaking Back, and Being Strategic

What Boomer would have been drawn to, in particular, was the value and the necessity of taking on prevailing discourses and reading them against the grain, re-working and even re-writing them. Hence, referring to his experience in the senior bureaucracy in South Australia, he spoke about being increasingly constrained by the new re-structuring imperatives, which in hindsight were the first clear signs of neo-liberal take-over. He described these policy initiatives as powerful, top-down 'stories', which he and others had to contend with, in seeking to tell other stories. He was very much caught in the middle, in the in-between. He was also under scrutiny and even attack, not just from below but from above as well. This is how he put it:

> I'm being told that I must tell my story, so I've got a choice, do I just lie down and tell the story, do I resist the story, or do I try to co-opt the story in some way[?] And a bit like Scheherazade, tell an acceptable version of the story which gives me room to live again to tell another story, and so it's a very awkward time for me in that regard.
>
> (Boomer, 1992d, p. 40)

The problem was always: which story does he go with, and support? – the 'powerful' story from above, the counter-story from below, or his own, which is neither one nor the other, but a tale personally forged over a long time of struggling towards authoritative agency. Elsewhere he writes: "I believe strategists for change need to exploit the rhetoric and accentuate the reforming tendencies immanent in new proposals" (Boomer, 1999a, p. 122). This means being both aware of and knowledgeable about rhetoric itself – from one perspective, the art of persuasion – and capable of re-working prevailing policy, as itself a form of rhetoric. As he points out, policies are documented, and available publicly, in one form or another. They can be worked with, and read with *and* against the grain, even in the heat of the moment. Like all texts, they are open to interpretation, though of course this work is never as easy as that sounds, given the nature of policy and policy-regimes. The challenge is to pick out the positive and contradictory moments in official discourse. As Boomer writes, apropos of the dominant policy directions of his day:

> [T]o better understand how one might use the power of these new dispensations, one needs to realise that the new policy documents themselves are conflicted and often schizoid, being the result of national negotiation, and therefore, in order to appease various interests and orientations, having had to accommodate autocratic and democratic orientations and shades of grey in between. One will accordingly find in national statements both conservation of a 'discipline' approach and encouragement for processing, enquiry and critique.
> (Boomer, 1999a, p. 122)

This is clearly (counter-)hegemonic work, and Boomer was certainly aware of Gramsci's theory of hegemony, although he acknowledged he was still coming to terms with it.[6] The point is he was *practising* it, seeking to dis-articulate and rearticulate policy's discursive features and elements. This is something that often needs to be done on the run, in (reflective) practice, and is perhaps part of what being a pragmatic-radical professional involves – something one *learns*, and a knowledge-ability one develops over time. It is also likely to be exhausting, and stressful – and clearly it was for Boomer.

It is nonetheless the kind of necessary, strategic mindset that is needed in difficult circumstances. Boomer was well aware of this, and of its costs and consequences. He was himself a target, and he knew it, as he commented late in his career, from his now senior vantage-point and continuing the story theme introduced above, about "being co-opted into a story" that he "didn't particularly want to be co-opted into" (Boomer, 1992d, p. 42). It is difficult, indeed, to avoid being co-opted in some fashion in the educational world we find ourselves in, at various levels of participation, and so there is likely to be for many a shock of recognition in formulations such as this, not simply in the present but over the past 30 years or so.

In Defence of Teachers

But it is what has happened to the profession that would most particularly disappoint Boomer, as a constant champion of teachers and teaching, and of *English* teaching at its best, as he thought it should and could be. How is it that many teachers have become so disillusioned and demoralised, so much under the hammer, reduced in various ways to objects of policy, and (re)constructed as technicians and implementers, operating within what is now a pervasive bureaucratic-professional frame? This was something he recognised in his own time and context, as emergent in education culture. Teaching was being 'recruited' by what would become neoliberalism, and redefined, re-positioned. In 1988, with greater knowledge of what was happening elsewhere, on top of what he knew of Australia, he described teaching as "at the crossroads", internationally. As he wrote: "Much of what I see in the USA provides the grimmest warning about what can happen if teachers construe themselves, in response to political/societal conditioning, as functionaries and technicians" (Boomer, 1999f, p. 33). In what still rings true, and loud and clear, in the educational landscape of the 21st century, he described the situation in Australia as one in which "teacher morale and self-esteem is falling in the face of an unremitting denigration of public schooling trumpeted in the media and reflected in educational budgets" (p. 33).[7] Moreover, 'teacher-bashing' was rife, and remains so (Mockler, 2022). Hence, he argued, we needed to find ways of changing the *conditions* of teaching, as well as its forms and features, mindful of a changing world, and of both "what is at stake" and, importantly, "what is entailed in the act of teaching, *beyond our specialism*" (p. 33).

In this latter point he was gesturing towards the need for due appreciation, on everyone's part – *including* teachers themselves – of the distinctive character of teaching. Being a *teacher*, that is, has priority over being a *teacher of* 'English', or whatever the subject-area may be. This distinction is undoubtedly a fine one, in practice, and the point itself needs to be carefully modulated.[8] Boomer saw the under-valuing of teachers and teaching as a matter for deep concern, not only for the profession but for the nation. He recognised the rolling-back of pedagogic possibility and the intractability of what he called the 'change problem' in education, claiming that "more radical solutions (in the sense of going to the root of the issue)" were needed. In his view, pedagogy was crucial in this regard:

> Unless we solve the pedagogy problem, all other efforts at reconstruction, including efforts to reconstruct the Australian workforce, will be in vain. The curriculum is, in the final instance, what teachers enact in classrooms. If we do not find ways of supporting and ensuring pedagogical change, we might as well save our money and efforts in other directions.
>
> (Boomer, 1999i, p. 136)

While he was referring to much more than 'English' teaching here, his point applies as much *if not more* to English teaching as to any other form of teaching at whatever level. Indeed, a case can be made that there are historical reasons why English teaching might be linked to primary teaching, as sites where there is a particular emphasis on the 'developmental' and 'interpersonal' functions of teaching and teachers' work (Connell, 1985). This risks, of course, perpetuating subject English's sense of 'exceptionalism'; but it is true nonetheless that one aspect of post-Dartmouth English teaching is its 'permeability', its openness to student experience, and to allowing the 'outside' in. Hence notions such as 'difficult knowledge' and 'funds of knowledge' may be particularly pertinent to English teaching, certainly in the post-Dartmouth tradition, in the sense that English teachers may well be more amenable to allowing opportunity for their expression in the classroom.

Performing Pedagogy, or the Larrikin Lessons

Worth returning to at this point, and re-emphasising, is the *performative* character of Boomer's work. As we saw in Chapter 4, he was drawn increasingly to enact his thinking and his theorising, to play it out in public, in the course and context of his presentations. The conference address was, indeed, a major forum for his ongoing work in this regard – at once the scene of pedagogy and the theatre of theory-in-the-making. He deliberately used such occasions as opportunities to engage and provoke, as much as to inform, and in this he was arguably unique among leading English teaching figures of his time, and possibly even since then, although perhaps more in *style* than anything else. It has been said of the Canadian curriculum scholar Ted Aoki that he approached conference keynotes and the like explicitly as *pedagogy*: "I know of no other scholar who took as seriously as Aoki did the scholarly conference as an educational event. Often working from conference themes Aoki takes these opportunities to teach, and with great savvy and subtlety" (Pinar, 2005, p. xv).[9] The same might be said of Boomer, and strikingly so.

He typically worked up the conference occasion as a pedagogic opportunity; indeed, the links between pedagogy and rhetoric, already mentioned, are worth re-acknowledging here. Where Boomer differed from Aoki, especially later in his career, was in his interest in exploring ways and means of foregrounding performance and artifice, and in playing with representation and its effects. This might be seen as a form of laying bare the device, the 'machinery'. Hence he would wear different hats, literally, to indicate that he was taking on different speaking-positions, 'staging' their differences.[10] Other strategies such as interruption – interrupting the flow, or the mimetic consistency of the fiction, the immersive pleasure of the narrative, the tale well-told, the enthralling drama – were also employed, increasingly with greater surety as he developed his Brechtian ethos, his own lived sense of the art and science of teaching, and the practised practice of his public pedagogy.

The problem is, of course, that performance of its very nature is ephemeral. It works in the moment, in the lived experience – much like action in the classroom, one might say. More often than not there are no traces left behind, no 'evidence', nothing one can return to and study, and render into conventional forms of scholarship. Sometimes there is an audio-visual record, but if there is, it tends to be of limited quality and value. Yet there can be no denying that performance has its own extraordinary power, at least potentially. It need not be 'theatrical', either, although it can be; and in Boomer's case, he was concerned on occasions to deliberately create anti-theatrical effects, aimed at breaking the illusion and challenging expectation. This was often quite humorous, too. He wasn't averse to playing the clown. From the outset, he had played with language – coining the term 'strugglish'[11] in an early paper (Boomer, 1988f), for instance, and even suggesting (tongue in cheek...) that English itself might be renamed as 'Strugglish'; or offering up the term 'curriculum-ing' to convey a more dynamic sense of 'curriculum', with its tendency to encourage a focus on nouns, things, fixities and unities, products and programmes, when he needed to or felt it appropriate. Hence, in his address to a 1992 NCTE conference in Washington, one of the 'voices' he evoked was clearly an old-school Australian teacher: "Blimey! Stone the crows! Would you believe it? Just what I need. Like a hole in the head" (Boomer, 1993, p. 4). This is clearly caricature, and it works – especially in the context of an Australian addressing an American conference! Although there are risks too, undoubtedly, and Boomer was keenly aware of this. Would everyone get the joke? Or see behind the surface appearance, or at least sense that something else was happening, or left unsaid? Perhaps it was time to get serious…

Yet it does seem warranted to evoke here the notion of Boomer as 'larrikin', an Australian expression that, while still somewhat ambivalent, is often mobilised to signify someone distinctively or recognisably 'Australian', which Boomer undoubtedly was. Wikipedia describes 'larrikin' thus: "an Australian English term meaning 'a mischievous young person, an uncultivated, rowdy but good hearted person', or 'a person who acts with apparent disregard for social or political conventions'". According to Google, it refers to "[a] person who acts with apparently careless disregard for social or political conventions; a person who is unsophisticated but likeable and good-hearted, 'a rough diamond'; a joker". Although it might seem gendered, and masculinist, this isn't at all necessarily the case, as it has been applied to both males and females (Bellanta, 2012). Perhaps another way of thinking about this is to relate it to the notion of 'taking the piss', often seen as a distinctive Australian attitude. Piss-taking is well described by Niall Lucy's (2010) deconstructive account of 'joking', with reference to the 2007 APEC summit in Sydney. He describes a satirical stunt by a group of comedians, who (in)famously infiltrated the cavalcade, right under the noses of the high-power security guards and in full view of the media. An account also of Derrida, poetry and Australian identity, Lucy's essay is about reading and textuality, and questions of authority and democracy.[12] Taking the piss, stirring things up, making fun of what otherwise presents as serious business… "To do so", Lucy writes, "is to mock authority, poking fun especially at its self-importance and always – always – with a straight face" (p. 101). This attitude is something I think Boomer would have appreciated, and readily recognised – notwithstanding the seriousness of the undertaking overall. It is another dimension of larrikinism, then: to play the fool, or "the piss-taking prankster" (p. 102). This doesn't mean he took education any the less seriously, either; quite the contrary. Rather, such an attitude was, as he saw it, an appropriate one for pragmatic-radical educators to take on in new Dark Times, when laughter (or poetry) might be an act of resistance or a sign of hope.

Again this is edgy, and – like pedagogy – it requires both tact and timing. There was always a larrikin quality to Boomer's persona and, by extension, his work, ranging from English teaching to the educational bureaucracy. (He was often referred to in such terms, in fact.[13]) Of course there were limits to how far he could go in the circumstances he found himself in, perhaps increasingly so. He was known nonetheless for his irreverence, his sense of humour, his playfulness, as well as his reflexiveness, and also his charisma (not unrelated, in fact, and which he was inclined to problematise and to 'deconstruct'). This again can be seen as part of Boomer's distinctiveness, linked to his Australianness, as a key figure in the field. Is the shift from a British (or perhaps an Anglo-American) centre of gravity to an

Australian one relevant here? A distinctively Australian manner – is this what characterises his work and his career?

Beyond English Teaching?

Although this book focuses on Boomer's contribution to English teaching and the language arts, his work in other areas and aspects of education also needs to be acknowledged. Reference has already been made to his work in curriculum inquiry. He provides a good base for developing a fuller account of the classroom-as-curriculum, as a distinct level of curriculum (Deng, 2011; Green, 2022). At the same time he indicates how this needs to be properly contextualised, describing 'curriculum' as "the ultimate realisation for a complex enactment involving global, national, state, school, community, teacher and student actors, in terms of what students come to think, believe, know, and do" (Boomer, 1999a, p. 124). This point was a direct reference to his "'cosmic egg' theory of curriculum" (p. 124), and his appreciation of the increasingly urgent need for what Reid (2019, p. xxi) calls "a new education narrative". To this end, Boomer extended his early thinking on what he called a 'verb' curriculum (i.e., curriculum as 'verb', rather than as 'noun') to propose something that would be:

> a 'key concern' curriculum underpinned by key questions for life on earth. It cuts across the 'verb' curriculum…, but it is premised on the notion that in order to come to understanding, for each area of key concern, there will be promiscuous employment of any of the known human ways of processing, exploring and investigating, and use of any relevant fact, knowledge or concept currently established under the discipline (or 'noun') curriculum.
>
> (p. 117)

As he goes on:

> The 'key concern' curriculum is an agenda for continuing student action-research at ever higher levels of abstraction, complexity and scope. It develops quite logically, I suggest, from the 'cosmic egg' of curriculum discussion. Its questions and concerns have to do with the survival of the species and the improvement of life on earth.
>
> (p. 117)

This greatly widens the scale and scope of education itself. There is a link to be made here to his earlier work on 'chunking' ("the making of theories, ideologies and beliefs") and "a future curriculum chunked first according to *process* and then directed towards gutsy content and issues", originally published in 1981 (Boomer, 1988f, p. 34). English, he notes, "would be particularly strong on chunking, symbol-making and decoding"[14] (p. 34). Such 'futures' thinking is always to be carefully managed, with due regard for the pragmatics of the present moment and the urgencies and contingencies of practice. But it is not to be denied, either, because the world *is* changing. "It seems that, far beyond English teaching, we are on the brink of a monumental paradigm shift" (Boomer, 1988b, p. 8), perhaps to be associated with an emergent postmodernity. This theme is touched on in Boomer's "Epic" essay (discussed in Chapter 3). It is what others have seen as the unsettling, and even the overturning, of the "Cartesian-Newtonian paradigm" (Tremmel, 2006). Boomer evokes leading-edge work in biology, physics, artificial intelligence, brain science, and technology, including bio-technologies, in this regard (p. 8). He points to scholars such as Constance Weaver (1985) exploring new ideas about "the parallels" of research in science and in reading and literary theory, and the emergence of what she calls an "organic" model of the universe, superseding mechanism (p. 12). He might also have looked to Moffett's later trajectory as a reference-point, something of which he was certainly well aware, and to Moffett's explorations over this same period of holism, meditation, spirituality, and the bicameral mind (Moffett, 1981, 1994).[15] The point is, Boomer was actively looking for ways of thinking differently about life, education and the universe at this point, and this may well have been at least one direction he would have headed, albeit with a sharper political edge. What might this have meant for English teaching and literacy education?

Boomer's interest in children's television proves a clue in this regard. He had a long-time involvement in the work of the Australian Children's Television Foundation, serving on its Board and later as Vice-President, from 1989 to his death in 1993. In particular, he took a key role in the making of *Lift Off*, an innovative programme aimed at children aged 3–8.[16] This was something he was passionate about, and it may have provided an alternative or parallel universe to his more formal educational undertakings. He gives an insight into this in his essay "Lifting Off; or Re-Imagining Curriculum?" (Boomer, 1999c). As he writes, at the very time when the nation seemed so much in crisis and stress:

> a major television program has been conceived, developed and brought to the point where it is being produced ready for showing in mid 1992. The program is *Lift Off*, and it promises to break new ground both in education and in children's television. It is a truly post-modern program in the sense of being multi-faceted, many-layered, and culturally diverse. It is global, rather than parochial. It spans generations and cultures, past, present and imagined future.
>
> (p. 16)

Informed by Howard Gardner's multiple intelligences theory, and bearing in mind that formal schooling in the past has "unfortunately tended to concentrate on linguistic and logico-mathematical development, often to the detriment of other dimensions" (p. 16), the innovative series deliberately sought to "present a program with high-octane learning potency across all the intelligences" (p. 16). Imagination and creativity were foregrounded, as first principles, and young children positioned and constructed as active, engaged learners *and* citizens. Boomer also affirms here the importance of *story*, describing stories as "a special way of thinking", and moreover "as the lifeblood of a nation: as a means for people to think about this culture, to interpret its past, and to imagine its future" (p. 18). Importantly, film and television, and media more generally, are seen as forms of curriculum in themselves, with curriculum understood once again as story – a familiar theme in this book. This essay provides further evidence, then, of Boomer's rich vision for the future of subject English, embracing electronic and popular culture and also, in various ways, re-articulating education and entertainment, and within a radical-pragmatic frame.

In Conclusion

Something else that needs to be considered here, finally, returns us to the question of curriculum biography and a gendered history. Is this just another professional history featuring a dead white male? All of those descriptors apply, certainly. He was undoubted a typical white middle-class man, a man of his time, and moreover from all reports enthusiastically heterosexual. Undoubtedly there are conflicts and inconsistencies in his work, as well as his persona, and contradictions and ambiguities in what I have called here his 'project'. There may also be a certain classically patriarchal character to his narrative, perhaps unavoidably, given the course of history. A more elaborated account would have brought out more of his collaborative work and his participation in the intersection of second-generation feminism and educational and social progressivism.[17] English teaching was changing, and he was part of that change, along with many others, men and women. This story still remains to be told. Even so, Garth Boomer's role and significance, as a key nodal point, needs to be highlighted.

Having a better sense of his *oeuvre*, in its overall (con)textuality, is likely to be helpful to scholars and practitioners in many fields: English teaching, curriculum and pedagogy, teacher professional development, and curriculum theory. There is much to be gained from exploring such issues in greater depth, or in building on the insights he generated and the arguments he developed and presented, across his working life. His early death robbed us all of what he might have achieved with even just 10 or 20 more years. Yet there is much to work with, regardless.

It is timely to be re-reading Boomer's work, then, with a view to drawing his ideas and proposals into English curriculum discussion and debate in the present conjuncture, where a very different vision of education, schooling, and the subject-area prevails, framed and constrained in accordance with the economic-rationalist imperatives and prejudices of global neoliberalism. The challenge now is one of reinventing subject English and re-envisioning English teaching. In that regard, Garth Boomer's work represents an important counter-narrative, and a rich resource for the future of English teaching, right across the post-imperial Anglophone world.

Notes

1 As Doecke and Breen (2013) write, this "means approaching language and other social phenomena as always exceeding our understanding, requiring us to engage in a process ... of a continual back and forth, of a dialectical play between our analytical

categories and a world that always escapes us in its fullness and complexity and continual movement" (pp. 303–304). They make this observation in the context of critiquing 'genre theory' in its effects on English teaching and writing pedagogy.
2 See Howie (2023) for a more extended account of this matter, working from a similar perspective to the discussion here.
3 In particular, this is to completely overlook the extensive work in English teaching that focuses on writing pedagogy, reaching back to the 1980 IFTE conference in Sydney (Arnold, 1983).
4 Cited from a photocopied note to Bill Corcoran, in Corcoran (1998).
5 It is worth noting that Boomer didn't have a PhD and so it is likely he didn't have first-hand experience of what at the time tended to be normal practice in doctoral supervision, certainly in the Anglo-Australian context. His MEd work at the London Institute of Education in 1972–1973 (Boomer, 1988b, p. 2) was probably rather different in this regard from the norm.
6 As he put it, "I am still learning how hegemony works, but I now know that top-down/bottom-up distinctions are dangerous and likely to be wrong" (Boomer, 1988a, p. 237).
7 It was in this context that he referred to work such as that of Tracy Kidder and others, often of a journalistic, popular character. He would have applauded recent Australian work in this vein, such as that of Gabbie Stroud. Stroud's memoir (2018) and subsequent novel (2023) powerfully convey the often intolerable pressures that contemporary teachers are encountering and why far too many (herself included) are leaving the profession.
8 There is no sense intended here that teaching can be somehow separated from 'content' – this is all the more important to note given contemporary curriculum debates about 'bringing knowledge back in' and new emphases on 'knowledge-led' curriculum work.
9 Other affinities with Aoki can be noted – for instance, the fact that they were working at much the same time, and that both evinced a deep commitment to school practitioners.
10 As Brock (2013, p. 18) writes: "I remember Garth speaking at one conference in which he tried to protect his neck by theatrically distinguishing between his 'public' and 'private' voices: Garth exuded theatricality! He had two hats sitting on the rostrum. If I remember correctly, one was white and the other black. He identified one of them as his public hat and the other as his private hat. At certain times in his speech, Garth put on his public or private hat as appropriate to what he was saying. If I remember correctly, most of what might be considered his more/most controversial declamations were issued with him wearing his private hat". This relates also, clearly, to Boomer's necessarily strategic involvement in bureaucracy and senior management, as outlined previously.
11 Boomer (1988f, p. 33) was quick to stress that he was concerned here with "*intentional* struggling, constructive struggling, concerned struggling, inspired by a kind of educational Darwinism".
12 As Lucy (2010) writes: "Nothing undermines the authority of the state, let alone the authority of authority, more so than too much reading" (p. 100). The essay is very appropriate, then, with regard to English teaching.
13 Consider the following from Wendy Morgan, for example, presented as a dedication to her well-received monograph on 'Ned Kelly', an Australian bushranger: "For Garth Boomer, who set me an example as a post-modern educator and a larrikin as game as Ned Kelly" (Morgan, 1992). She is well known for her work in critical literacy and English teaching (Misson & Morgan, 2006; Morgan, 1997), and, incidentally, was the "Real Respondent" in Boomer's Washington NCTE address (Boomer, 1993).
14 'Decoding' here, as Boomer put it, involves "interpreting cultures, literature, media, societies, human behaviours, political parties, languages, dialects, etc." (p. 34)!
15 See Marine et al. (2023) for recent re-evaluations of Moffett's later work, which hitherto has tended to be viewed with great scepticism in the field, and indeed as a 'New Age' cul-de-sac. Today's concern with climate change and other global

emergencies is forcing new thinking right across the board, including – somewhat belatedly – education. Regarding recent re-appraisals of Moffett more generally, see Blau et al. (2023).
16 It is little-known, too, that Boomer's involvement extended to scriptwriting and the like, with Reid (2017) noting that he "used his creative-writing talents and his understanding of learning and teaching to contribute" to the programme.
17 Recent Australian work (e.g., McLeod, 2014; McLeod & Paisley, 2023; cf. Fallace, 2015) explores these issues, broadening the educational discussion well beyond English teaching, and providing a revisionary and situated account of 'progressivism' (see also Green, 2021b).

Appendix: Ten Strategies for Good Teaching

As a summary I will offer ten general principles or broad strategies that emerge from the practices described in Sections 1, 2 and 3 [i.e., the original *Negotiating the Curriculum* book]. Using these strategies, teachers can generate an infinite number of teaching sequences within the framework of a negotiated curriculum.

Apprenticeship

The teacher is senior reader of the school culture and special senior reader of the specialist subculture of the subject. Wittingly or unwittingly, he/she is demonstrating how to be a reader and maker of meaning. I suggest that this should be taught self-consciously and wittingly. Students should be shown in detail how to do it, and the showing should be accompanied by anecdote and recollection about how it was learnt and overcome, whatever 'it' may be (spelling a word, handling a plane, solving a problem, thinking through a theorem, etc.).

Bushcraft

In the ecology of the school 'bush' there is a bewildering array of texts, tests, assignments and artefacts. The teacher should be used to finding interesting and pertinent specimens and talking about their characteristics, habits and habitats. Students should be encouraged to familiarise themselves with funny creatures, like science textbooks, learning how to tame them, remembering where the dangers lurk and noting little peculiarities.

Telling Secrets

This is where teachers can 'come clean' about short cuts, various other ways of doing something, and mistakes they have made themselves. It is also where students can be encouraged, in a supportive group, to talk about their learning mazes and journeys, 'warts and all'. Thus the precious underground of school culture can be shared, to empower and enrich each mind.

Transforming

Bruner has said that schools should be on about the acquisition of skilled performance in culturally important media. He has also said that each time one transforms knowledge or explores a certain territory in a new medium, the knowledge is intensified. Whatever we want children to *know* should, by this dictum, be subjected to study through a variety of media (talk, photography, writing, drama, painting, modelling, etc.). Transforming something from talk into, say, writing requires a more rigorous attention to meaning and various forms of translation. Transforming is a mind-stretching, empowering activity central to the 'reading' process.

Connecting

The more richly a teacher can spin a tapestry of metaphor and analogy into a 'thick' redundant text of thinking about something new, the more likely it is that students will find a way in. If students are encouraged to spin out reciprocally their own webs of anecdote, metaphor and analogy, it is less likely that some will remain outside the next text. The art of generating apt analogy and metaphor is central to the 'reading' teacher's task.

Imagining

If students cannot imagine the likely benefits of learning and entering a new 'culture', they will not *intend* to journey, and any learning will be 'welded on', 'dinned in', and therefore precarious. Before 'entering' a new text or a new concept or a new skill with students, teachers should be obliged to ensure that students can imagine themselves beneficially 'doing it' at some future date.

Guessing

Once students intend and feel that they have a better-than-even chance, they will begin to punt with expectation. Through trial and error they will frame progressively better hypotheses. Teachers must encourage punting, risk-taking, error-making and tenacity. When students stop guessing, they stop learning.

Asking

If schools are to become more powerful institutions of learning, we must change the balance of 'question asking'. The amount of learning is directly proportional to the number of questions asked by the learner. If the teacher is asking all the questions, then by this formula, the teacher is doing most of the learning. Questions will come from learners if they intend and if they are puzzled. The question-asking balance will change as the teacher gets more children intending and arranges for them to be well-and-truly puzzled. Constructive contradiction is very important in this regard.

Producing

If reading and listening are seen as a *taking* and *building* of meaning, then to read and listen is to *produce*. Power comes through production, not through receiving. Reception can provide fuel for production. One reads the culture so that one can *act* upon it and indeed re-write parts of it. A vigorous teacher will always be pushing students into the productive mode, towards the ultimate public *test*. Until they can do something or apply it, it is academic.

Reflecting

It is a human trait to love the indwelling re-creation of the journey, the lingering on good passages, the exorcising of the disturbing. Through reflection we confirm our learning and learn how to do it better next time. Schools in Australia are uncivil in the haste with which they race from test to the next journey. Any learning theorist, indeed any sensible person, will say that celebrating through reflection is an essential feature of human life. We all need to feel the quality.

References

AERO (2022). *Writing and Writing Instruction: An Overview of the Literature*, Adelaide: Australian Educational Research Organisation (February).
AERO (2023). *Supporting Students Significantly Behind in Literacy and Numeracy: A Review of Evidence-Based Approaches*, Adelaide: Australian Educational Research Organisation (May).
Anson, D.W.J. (2021). "'That's Deep Bro': Negotiated Readings and Democratic Education in an Australian High School Classroom", *Discourse: Studies in the Cultural Politics of Education*, Vol. 42, No. 6, pp. 930–942. doi:10.1080/01596306.2020.1774744.
Apple, M.W. & Beane, J.A. (Eds.) (2007). *Democratic Schools: Lessons in Powerful Education*, 2nd Edition, Portsmouth, NH: Heinemann Educational Books.
Arnold, R. (Ed.) (1983). *Timely Voices: English Teaching in the Eighties*, Melbourne: Oxford University Press.
Baker, J. (2020). "Teachers Fear They Lack Skills in Writing", *Sydney Morning Herald*, September 16, p. 1/p. 8.
Ball, S.J. (1985). "English for the English since 1906", in I.F. Goodson (Ed.), *Social Histories of the Secondary Curriculum: Subjects for Study*, London & Philadelphia: The Falmer Press, pp. 53–88.
Barnes, D. (1976). *From Communication to Curriculum*, Harmondsworth: Penguin Books.
Barnes, D. & Barnes, D. (1983). "Cherishing Private Souls? Writing in Fifth Year English Classes", in R. Arnold (Ed.), *Timely Voices: English Teaching in the Eighties*, Melbourne: Oxford University Press, pp. 35–51.
Barnes, D. & Barnes, D. (1986). "English as Action", *English in Australia*, Vol. 78, September, pp. 3–14.
Barnes, D., Britton, J. & Rosen, H. (1969). *Language, the Learner and the School*, Harmondsworth: Penguin Books.
Barrs, M. (2021). *Vygotsky the Teacher*, London & New York: Routledge.
Bellanta, M. (2012). *Larrikins: A History*, Brisbane: University of Queensland Press.
Benjamin, W. (1983). *Understanding Brecht*, London: Verso.
Bennington, G. (1997). "Politics and Friendship: A Discussion with Jacques Derrida", Centre for Modern French Thought, University of Sussex, 1 December. www.livingphilosophy.org/Derrida-politics-friendship.htm
Bernstein, B. (1977). "Class and Pedagogies: Visible and Invisible", in B. Bernstein, *Class, Codes and Control*, Vol. 3, 2nd Edition, London: Routledge & Kegan Paul, pp. 116–146.
Blacker, D.I. (2017). "The Politics of Recitation: Ideology, Interpellation, and Hegemony", *Harvard Educational Review*, Vol. 87, No. 3, pp. 357–379.

References

Blau, S., Kelly, K., Marine, J. & Rogers, P.M. (Eds) (2023). *The Legacy of James Moffett: His Shaping Influence on Writing Studies, English Education, and the Teaching of English*, Urbana, IL: National Council of Teachers of English (NCTE).

Boomer, G. (1973). "Coming of Age in Australia", in N. Bagnall (Ed.), *New Movements in the Study and Teaching of English*, London: Temple Smith, pp. 63–77.

Boomer, G. (1974/2010). "Eternal Triangles: Language and Literature in Senior English", *mETAphor*, Iss. 4, pp. 36–43 (Orig. pub. *The Teaching of English*, ETANSW, 1974).

Boomer, G. (1976). "Who's Afraid of the Illiteracy Scare? A Personal View", in G. Boomer & D. Spender, *The Spitting Image: Reflections on Language, Education and Class*, Adelaide: Rigby, pp. 124–131.

Boomer, G. (1977). "Secondary English – Yesterday, Today and Tomorrow", in K.D. Watson & R.D. Eagleson (Eds), *English in Secondary Schools: Today and Tomorrow*, Sydney: English Teachers' Association of NSW, pp. 1–17.

Boomer, G. (1978). "Negotiating the Curriculum", *English in Australia*, Vol. 44, June, pp. 16–29.

Boomer, G. (1982a). "Ten Strategies for Good Teaching", in G. Boomer (Ed.), *Negotiating the Curriculum: A Teacher-Student Partnership*, Sydney: Ashton-Scholastic, pp. 119–121. [See Appendix – this volume]

Boomer, G. (Ed.) (1982b). *Negotiating the Curriculum*. Sydney: Ashton Scholastic.

Boomer, G. (1982c). "The English Teacher, Research and Change (1966–1980)", in R.D. Eagleson (Ed.), *English in the Eighties*, Adelaide: Australian Association for the Teaching of English (AATE), pp. 134–145.

Boomer, G. (1982c). "Turning on the Learning Power: Introductory Notes", in G. Boomer (Ed.), *Negotiating the Curriculum: A Teacher-Student Partnership*, Sydney: Ashton-Scholastic, pp. 2–7.

Boomer, G. (1983). "*Towards a Science of English Teaching*", unpublished paper, presented at the National Conference of the Canadian Council for the Teaching of English (CCTE), Montreal, May.

Boomer, G. (1984). "Space and Meta Space", *Curriculum Perspectives*, Vol. 4, No. 2, pp. 57–59.

Boomer, G. (1985a). "The Wisdom of the Antipodes: What's Working for Literacy in Australia", in G. Boomer, *Fair Dinkum Teaching and Learning: Reflections on Literacy and Power*, Montclair, NJ: Boynton/Cook, pp. 190–204.

Boomer, G. (1985b). "Addressing the Problem of Elsewhereness: A Case for Action Research in Schools", in G. Boomer, *Fair Dinkum Teaching and Learning: Reflections on Literacy and Power*, Montclair, NJ: Boynton/Cook, pp. 122–129.

Boomer, G. (1985c). *Fair Dinkum Teaching and Learning: Reflections on Literacy and Power*, Montclair, NJ: Boynton/Cook.

Boomer, G. (1985d). "Language, Literature and Human Values", in S. Tchudi (Ed.), *Language, Schooling and Society*, Upper Montclair, NJ: Boynton/Cook Publishers, pp. 160–176.

Boomer, G. (1985e). "Becoming the Reader Over One's Own Shoulder", in G. Boomer, *Fair Dinkum Teaching and Learning: Reflections on Literacy and Power*, Montclair, NJ: Boynton/Cook, pp. 37–52.

Boomer, G. (1985f). "Towards a Model of the Composing Process in Writing", in G. Boomer, *Fair Dinkum Teaching and Learning: Reflections on Literacy and Power*, Montclair, NJ: Boynton/Cook, pp. 131–151.

Boomer, G. (1985g). "English Teaching: Art and Science", in S. Tchudi (Ed.), *Language, Schooling and Society*, Upper Montclair, NJ: Boynton/Cook Publishers, pp. 101–118.

Boomer, G. (1987a). "Creativity in Education: Making Things", in G. Boomer, *Changing Education: Reflections on National Issues in Education in Australia*, Canberra: Commonwealth Schools Commission, pp. 117–127.

Boomer, G. (1987b). "The Newspaper and Cultural Literacy", in G. Boomer, *Changing Education: Reflections on National Issues in Education in Australia*, Canberra: Commonwealth Schools Commission, pp. 47–55.

Boomer, G. (1988a). "Negotiating the System: A Letter to James Britton", in M. Lightfoot & N. Martin (Eds), *The Word for Teaching is Learning: Language and Learning Today – Essays for James Britton*, London: Heineman & Portsmouth, NH: Boynton/Cook, pp. 231–241.

Boomer, G. (1988b). "Dancing Lessons: An Introduction", in B. Green (Ed.), *Metaphors and Meanings: Essays on English Teaching by Garth Boomer*, Adelaide: Australian Association for the Teaching of English (AATE), pp. 1–12.

Boomer, G. (1988c). "Negotiation Revisited", in B. Green (Ed.), *Metaphors and Meanings: Essays on English Teaching by Garth Boomer*, Adelaide: Australian Association for the Teaching of English (AATE), pp. 168–178.

Boomer, G. (1988d). "Reading the Whole Curriculum", in B. Green (Ed.), *Metaphors and Meanings: Essays on English Teaching by Garth Boomer*, Adelaide: Australian Association for the Teaching of English (AATE), pp. 151–167.

Boomer, G. (1988e). "Teachers Learning", in B. Green (Ed.), *Metaphors and Meanings: Essays on English Teaching by Garth Boomer*, Adelaide: Australian Association for the Teaching of English (AATE), pp. 195–225.

Boomer, G. (1988f). "Struggling in English", in B. Green (Ed.), *Metaphors and Meanings: Essays on English Teaching by Garth Boomer*, Adelaide: Australian Association for the Teaching of English (AATE), pp. 31–41.

Boomer, G. (1988g). "Teaching Against the Grain", in B. Green (Ed.), *Metaphors and Meanings: Essays on English Teaching by Garth Boomer*, Adelaide: Australian Association for the Teaching of English (AATE), pp. 179–191.

Boomer, G. (1988h). "English Teaching: Art and Science", in B. Green (Ed.), *Metaphors and Meanings: Essays on English Teaching by Garth Boomer*, Adelaide: Australian Association for the Teaching of English (AATE), pp. 80–98.

Boomer, G. (1988i). "The English Teacher, Research and Change", in B. Green (Ed.), *Metaphors and Meanings: Essays on English Teaching by Garth Boomer*, Adelaide: Australian Association for the Teaching of English (AATE), pp. 15–30.

Boomer, G. (1988j). "Literature and English Teaching: Opening Up the Territory" in B. Green (Ed.), *Metaphors and Meanings: Essays on English Teaching by Garth Boomer*, Adelaide: Australian Association for the Teaching of English (AATE), pp. 99–108.

Boomer, G. (1988k). "The Politics of Drama Teaching", in B. Green (Ed.), *Metaphors and Meanings: Essays on English Teaching by Garth Boomer*, Adelaide: Australian Association for the Teaching of English (AATE), pp. 55–67.

Boomer, G. (1989). "*Literacy: The Epic Challenge beyond Progressivism*", Keynote Address to the Joint Annual Conference of Australian Reading Association and the Australian Association for the Teaching of English, Darwin, Australia, July. First published in *English in Australia* (Vol. 98, pp. 6–17) and then in Green (1999).

Boomer, G. (1992a). "Negotiating the Curriculum", in G. Boomer et al. (Eds), *Negotiating the Curriculum: Educating for the 21st Century*, London & Washington, DC: The Falmer Press, pp. 4–14.

Boomer, G. (1992b). "Negotiating the Curriculum Reformulated", in G. Boomer et al. (Eds), *Negotiating the Curriculum: Educating for the 21st Century*, London & Washington, DC: The Falmer Press, pp. 276–289.

Boomer, G. (1992c). "Curriculum Composing and Evaluating: An Invitation to Action Research", in G. Boomer et al. (Eds), *Negotiating the Curriculum: Educating for the 21st Century*, London & Washington, DC: The Falmer Press, pp. 32–45.

Boomer, G. (1992d). "Mapping the Terrain: An Interview with Garth Boomer", in *Changing Curriculum; Study Materials*, ECT436/736, Geelong, Victoria: Deakin University, Interviewers: B. Green & R. Walker, pp. 25–42.

Boomer, G. (1992e). "Advent of Standards in Australian Education", *Curriculum Perspectives*, Vol. 12, No. 1, pp. 61–66.

Boomer, G. (1993). "How to Make a Teacher", *English Education*, Vol. 25, No. 1, pp. 3–18.

Boomer, G. (1999a). "Changing Curriculum", in B. Green (Ed.), *Designs on Learning: Essays on Curriculum and Teaching by Garth Boomer*, Canberra: Australian Curriculum Studies Association (ACSA), pp. 113–126.

Boomer, G. (1999b). "Pragmatic-Radical Teaching and the Disadvantaged Schools Program", in B. Green (Ed.), *Designs on Learning: Essays on Curriculum and Teaching by Garth Boomer*, Canberra: Australian Curriculum Studies Association (ACSA), pp. 49–58.

Boomer, G. (1999c). "Lifting Off; or Re-Imagining Curriculum?" in B. Green (Ed.), *Designs on Learning: Essays on Curriculum and Teaching by Garth Boomer*, Canberra: Australian Curriculum Studies Association (ACSA), pp. 15–20.

Boomer, G. (1999d). "Democracy, Bureaucracy and the Classroom", in B. Green (Ed.), *Designs on Learning: Essays on Curriculum and Teaching by Garth Boomer*, Canberra: Australian Curriculum Studies Association (ACSA), pp. 101–112.

Boomer, G. (1999e). "What Are Teachers Up To? Speculating About the Secret Service", in B. Green (Ed.), *Designs on Learning: Essays on Curriculum and Teaching by Garth Boomer*, Canberra: Australian Curriculum Studies Association (ACSA), pp. 37–48.

Boomer, G. (1999f). "The Helping Hand Strikes Again: On Language, Learning and Teaching", in B. Green (Ed.), *Designs on Learning: Essays on Curriculum and Teaching by Garth Boomer*, Canberra: Australian Curriculum Studies Association (ACSA), pp. 23–35.

Boomer, G. (1999g). "Literacy: The Epic Challenge Beyond Progressivism", in B. Green (Ed.), *Designs on Learning: Essays on Curriculum and Teaching by Garth Boomer*, Canberra: Australian Curriculum Studies Association (ACSA), pp. 83–98.

Boomer, G. (1999h). "Education and the Media – Makers or Mirrors? Dilemmas in the Development of Australian Culture", in B. Green (Ed.), *Designs on Learning: Essays on Curriculum and Teaching by Garth Boomer*, Canberra: Australian Curriculum Studies Association (ACSA), pp. 71–81.

Boomer, G. (1999i). "Curriculum and Teaching in Australian School 1969–1980: A Tale of Two Epistemologies", in B. Green (Ed.), *Designs on Learning: Essays on Curriculum and Teaching by Garth Boomer*, Canberra: Australian Curriculum Studies Association (ACSA), pp. 127–146.

Boomer, G. & Spender, D. (1976). *The Spitting Image: Reflections on Language, Education and Class*, Adelaide: Rigby.

Boomer, G. & Torr, H. (1987). "Becoming a Powerful Teacher", in B. Comber & J. Hancock (Eds), *Developing Teachers: A Celebration of Teachers' Learning in Australia*, North Ryde: Methuen Australia, pp. 2–10.

Boomer, G., Lester, N., Onore, C. & Cook, J. (Eds) (1992). *Negotiating the Curriculum: Educating for the 21st Century*, London & Washington, DC: The Falmer Press.

References

Brennan, M., Mayes, E. & Zipin, L. (2022). "The Contemporary Challenge of Activism as Curriculum Work", *Journal of Educational Administration and History*, Vol. 54, No. 3, pp. 319–333. https://doi.org/10.1080/00220620.2020.1866508.

Britton, J. (1966). *"What Is English?" Working Papers of the Anglo-American Seminar on the Teaching and Learning of English*. Dartmouth College, Hanover, New Hampshire, August 20 – September 16, pp. 1–14. https://files.eric.ed.gov/fulltext/ED082201.pdf.

Britton, J. (1970). *Language and Learning*, Harmondsworth: Penguin Books.

Britton, J. (1973). "How We Got Here", in N. Bagnall (Ed.), *New Movements in the Study and Teaching of English*, London: Temple Smith, pp. 13–29.

Britton, J. (1977). "Language and the Nature of Learning: An Individual Perspective", in J. R. Squire (Ed.), *The Teaching of English: The Seventy-Sixth Yearbook of the National Society for the Study of Education, Part I*. Chicago: University of Chicago Press, pp. 1–38.

Britton, J. (1982). "English Teaching: Retrospect and Prospect", in R.D. Eagleson (Ed.), *English in the Eighties*, Adelaide: Australian Association for the Teaching of English, pp. 1–12. Reprinted in G. Pradl (Ed.) (1982), *Prospect and Retrospect: Selected Essays of James Britton*, Montclair, NJ: Boynton/Cook Publishers & London: Heinemann Educational, pp. 201–215.

Britton, J. (1986). "Attempting to Clarify Our Objectives for Teaching English", *English Education*, Vol. 18, No. 3, pp. 153–158.

Britton, J., Burgess, T., Martin, N., McLeod, A. & Rosen, H. (1975). *The Development of Writing Abilities (11–18)*, London: Macmillan Education.

Brock, P. (2013). "In Memory of Garth Boomer: May he not 'rust unburnished' but 'shine in use'", *English in Australia*, Vol. 48, No. 3, pp. 12–20. [NB: originally presented in 2005]

Bron, J., Bovill, C. & Veugelers, W. (2022). "Students Experiencing and Developing Democratic Citizenship Through Curriculum Negotiation: The Relevance of Garth Boomer's Approach", *Curriculum Perspectives*, Vol. 42, pp. 39–49. https://doi.org/10.1007/s41297-021-00155-3.

Burgess, T. (1988). "On Difference: Cultural and Linguistic Diversity and English Teaching", in M. Lightfoot & N. Martin (Eds), *The Word for Teaching is Learning: Language and Learning Today – Essays for James Britton*, London: Heineman & Portsmouth, NH: Boynton/Cook, pp. 155–168.

Campbell, A. & Groundwater-Smith, S. (Eds) (2009). *Connecting Inquiry and Professional Learning in Education: International Perspectives and Practical Solutions*, London: Routledge.

Clary, D. & Mueller, F. (2021). *Writing Matters: Reversing a Legacy of Policy Failure in Australian Education*, Sydney: The Centre for Independent Studies, Analysis Paper 23.

Collins, C. (1995). "Curriculum Stocktake: A Context", in C. Collins (Ed.), *Curriculum Stocktake: Evaluating School Curriculum Change*, Canberra: The Australian College of Education, pp. 3–19.

Comber, B. (2013). "Teachers as Researchers: A 'Fair Dinkum' Learning Legacy", *English in Australia*, Vol. 48, No. 3, pp. 53–61.

Comber, B. (2016). *Literacy, Place and Pedagogies of Possibility*, New York & London: Routledge.

Connell, R. (1985). *Teachers' Work*, Sydney: George Allen & Unwin.

Cook, J. (1992). "Negotiating the Curriculum: Programming for Learning", in G. Boomer, N. Lester, C. Onore & J. Cook (Eds), *Negotiating the Curriculum: Educating for the 21st Century*, London & Washington, DC: The Falmer Press, pp. 15–31.

Cook-Sather, A. (2006). "Sound, Presence and Power: 'Student Voice' in Educational Research and Reform", *Curriculum Inquiry*, Vol. 36, No. 4, pp. 359–390.

Corcoran, B. (1998). "Facing Up to Boomer's 'Epic Challenge': The Progressives Under Fire – *English in Australia* 1990-1996", *English in Australia*, Vol. 122, pp. 104–117.

Crowley, T. (2018). "Marx, Volosinov, Williams: Language, History, Practice", *Language Sciences*, Vol. 70, pp. 37–44.

Cuban, L. (1984). *How Teachers Taught: Constancy and Change in American Schools 1890-1980*, New York & London: Teachers College Press.

Dellit, J. (2011). "The Quest for Quality and Equity in [South Australian] Curriculum", in L. Yates, C. Collins & K. O'Connor (Eds), *Australia's Curriculum Dilemmas: State Cultures and the Big Picture*, Melbourne: Melbourne University Press, pp. 148-162.

Deng, Z. (2011). "Revisiting Curriculum Potential", *Curriculum Inquiry*, Vol. 4, No. 5, pp. 538–559.

Derrida, J. (1978). "Structure, Sign and Play in the Discourse of the Human Sciences", in *Writing and Difference*, trans. with an Introduction and Additional Notes, by Alan Bass, London & Henley: Routledge & Kegan Paul, pp. 278–293.

Derrida, J. (2002). "The Deconstruction of Actuality", in J. Derrida, *Negotiations: Interventions and Interviews, 1971–2001*, Trans. and Intro. E. Rottenberg, Stanford, CA: Stanford University Press.

Dixon, J. (1975). *Growth Through English – Set in the Context of the Seventies*, London: Oxford University Press for the National Association for the Teaching of English.

Doecke, B. & Breen, L. (2013). "Beginning Again: A Response to Rosen and Christie", *Changing English*, Vol. 20, No. 3, pp. 292–305. doi:10.1080/1358684X.2013.816531.

Doecke, B. & Mirhosseini, S.-A. (2023). "Multiple Englishes: Multiple Ways of Being in the World (A Conversational Inquiry)", *English in Education*, Vol. 57, No. 2, pp. 76–90. doi:10.1080/04250494.2023.2189910.

Doll, W.E. (1993). *A Post-Modern Perspective on Curriculum*, New York & London: Teachers College Press.

Durst, R.K. (2015). "British Invasion: James Britton, Composition Studies, and Anti-Disciplinarity", *College Composition and Communication*, Vol. 66, No. 3, pp. 384–401.

Egan, K. (1986). *Teaching as Storytelling: An Alternative Approach to Teaching and the Curriculum*, London: Routledge.

Egéa-Kuehne, D. (2003). "The Teaching of Philosophy: Renewed Rights and Responsibilities", *Educational Philosophy and Theory*, Vol. 35, No. 3, pp. 271–284.

Elliott, J. (1998). "The Teacher's Role in Curriculum Development: An Unresolved Issue in English Attempts at Curriculum Reform", in J. Elliot, *The Curriculum Experiment: Meeting the Challenge of Social Change*, Milton Keynes: Open University Press, pp. 17–41.

Eyers, S. & Richmond, J. (2012). "Preface to the Second Edition", in *Becoming Our Own Experts: The Vauxhall Papers – Studies of Language and Learning made by the Talk Workshop Group at Vauxhall Manor School, 1974–1979*, London: www.becomingourownexperts.org.

Fallace, T.D. (2015). *Race and the Origins of Progressive Education, 1880–1929*, New York: Teachers College Press.

Frow, J. (2007). "Australian Cultural Studies: Theory, Story, History", *Postcolonial Studies*, Vol. 10, No. 1, pp. 59–75.

Gannon, S. (2019). "Teaching Writing in the NAPLAN Era: The Experiences of Secondary English Teachers", *English in Australia*, Vol. 4, No. 2, pp. 43–56.

Giroux, H.A. (1988). *Teachers as Intellectuals: Toward a Critical Pedagogy of Learning*, Massachusetts, MA: Bergin & Garvey Publishers.

Green, B. (1987). "Gender, Genre and Writing Pedagogy", in I. Reid (Ed.), *The Place of Genre in Learning: Current Debates*, Geelong, Victoria: Centre for Studies in Literary Education, Deakin University, pp. 83–90.

Green, B. (Ed.) (1988). *Metaphors and Meanings: Essays on English Teaching by Garth Boomer*, Adelaide: Australian Association for the Teaching of English (AATE).

Green, B. (1990a). "Imagining the Curriculum: Programming for Meaning in Subject English", *English in Australia*, Vol. 94, pp. 39–58.

Green, B. (1990b). "A Dividing Practice: 'Literature', English Teaching and Cultural Politics", in I. Goodson & P. Medway (Eds), *Bringing English to Order: The History and Politics of a School Subject*, London & Washington, DC: The Falmer Press, pp. 135–161.

Green, B. (1995a). "*Metaphors and Monsters, or After the New English?*" Keynote Address at the Conference of the International Association for the Teaching of English, New York. www.researchgate.net/publication/368360980_METAPHORS_AND_MONSTERS_OR_AFTER_THE_NEW_ENGLISH.

Green, B. (1995b). "Post-Curriculum Possibilities: English Teaching, Cultural Politics, and the Postmodern Turn", *Journal of Curriculum Studies*, Vol. 27, No. 4, pp. 391–409.

Green, B. (1998). "Born Again Teaching? Governmentality, 'Grammar' and Public Schooling", in T.S. Popkewitz & M. Brennan (Eds), *Foucault's Challenge: Discourse, Knowledge, and Power in Education*, New York: Teachers College Press, pp. 173–204.

Green, B. (1999). "Garth Boomer – Curriculum Worker for the Nation", in B. Green (Ed.), *Designs on Learning: Essays on Curriculum and Teaching by Garth Boomer*, Canberra: Australian Curriculum Studies Association (ACSA), pp. 1–12.

Green, B. (2003a). "Unfinished Business? Garth Boomer and the Pedagogical Imagination", *Opinion: Journal of the South Australian English Teachers' Association*, Vol. 47, No. 2, pp. 13–24.

Green, B. (2003b). "Curriculum Inquiry in Australia: Towards a Local Genealogy of the Curriculum Field", in W.F. Pinar (Ed.), *Handbook of International Curriculum Research*, Mahwah, NJ: Lawrence Erlbaum Associates, pp. 123–141.

Green, B. (2006). "English, Literacy, Rhetoric: Changing the Project?" *English in Education*, Vol. 40, No. 1, pp. 7–19.

Green, B. (Ed.) (2009). *Understanding and Researching Professional Practice*, Rotterdam: Sense Publishers.

Green, B. (2018a). "Curriculum Studies in Australia: Stephen Kemmis and the Deakin Legacy", in C. Edwards-Groves, P. Grootenboer & J. Wilkinson (Eds), *Education in an Era of Schooling: Critical Perspectives of Educational Practice and Action Research – A Festschrift for Stephen Kemmis*, Singapore: Springer, pp. 27–45.

Green, B. (2018b). "From Communication Studies to Curriculum Inquiry?" in B. Green, *Engaging Curriculum: Bridging the Curriculum Theory and English Education Divide*, London & New York: Routledge, pp. 84–99.

Green, B. (2018c). *Engaging Curriculum: Bridging the Curriculum Theory and English Education Divide*, London & New York: Routledge.

Green, B. (2021a). "Re-Negotiating the Curriculum?" *Curriculum Perspectives*, Vol. 41, pp. 213–225. https://doi.org/10.1007/s41297-021-00143-7.

Green, B. (2021b). "Curriculum History and Progressive Education in Australia: A Prolegomenon", in B. Green, P. Roberts & M. Brennan (Eds), *Curriculum Challenges and Opportunities in a Changing World: Transnational Perspectives in Curriculum Inquiry*, New York: Palgrave Macmillan, pp. 197–216.

Green, B. (2022). "Understanding Curriculum as Practice, or On the Practice Turn(s) in Curriculum Inquiry", *Curriculum Perspectives*, Vol. 42, pp. 77–83. https://doi.org/10.1007/s41297-022-00160-0.

Green, B. (2023). "Margaret's Reading Lessons; or, Literature as Curriculum", *English in Education*, Vol. 57, No. 1, pp. 59–68.

Green, B. & Beavis, C. (1996). "Introduction: English Teaching and Curriculum History", in B. Green & C. Beavis (Eds), *Teaching the English Subjects: Essays on English Curriculum History and Australian Schooling*, Geelong, Victoria: Deakin University Press, pp. 1–14.

Green, B. & Beavis, C. (Eds) (2012). *Literacy in 3D: An Integrated Perspective in Theory and Practice*, Camberwell, Victoria: Australian Council for Educational Research.

Green, B. & Meiers, M. (2013). "Garth Boomer – 20 Years On", *English in Australia*, Vol. 48, No. 3, pp. 4–6. [NB: Editorial Statement]

Green, B. & Sawyer, W. (2023). "James Moffett in Australia: Writing Pedagogy and Post-Dartmouth English Teaching", in S. Blau, K. Kelly, J. Marine, & P.M. Rogers (Eds), *The Legacy of James Moffett: His Shaping Influence on Writing Studies, English Education, and the Teaching of English*, Urbana, IL: National Council of Teachers of English (NCTE) – in press (March, 2024).

Green, B., Hodgens, J. & Luke, A. (1997). "Debating Literacy in Australia? History Lessons and Popular F(r)ictions", *Australian Journal of Language and Literacy*, Vol. 20, No. 1, pp. 6–25.

Gusdorf, G. (1965). *Speaking*, Trans. and Intro. by P.T. Brockelman, Evanston, IL: Northwestern University Press.

Hardcastle, J. (1997). "History into Mind: English Teaching and the Idealist Legacy", *Changing English*, Vol. 4, No. 1, pp. 31–49. doi:10.1080/1358684970040103.

Hardcastle, J. (2009). "Vygotsky's Enlightenment Precursors", *Educational Review*, Vol. 61, No. 2, pp. 181–195.

Harris, J. (2012). *A Teaching Subject: Composition Since 1966*, Logan, UT: Utah State University Press.

Hicks, D. (2014). *The Road Out: A Teacher's Odyssey in Poor America*, Oakland, CA: University of California Press.

Hirsch, E.D. (1987). *Cultural Literacy: What Every American Needs to Know*, Boston, MA: Houghton Mifflin.

Homer, D. (1982). "English, Orthodoxy and the Eighties", in D. Mallick, P. Moss & I. Hansen (Eds), *New Essays in the Teaching of Literature*, Adelaide: Australian Association for the Teaching of English (AATE), pp. 75–83.

Homer, D. (2003). "Playing for the B Team: A Tale of the Eighties", in B. Doecke, D. Homer & H. Nixon (Eds), *English Teachers at Work: Narratives, Counter Narratives and Arguments*, Adelaide: Australian Association for the Teaching of English (AATE), pp. 206–225.

Hopmann, S. (2007). "Restrained Teaching: The Common Core of *Didaktik*", *European Educational Research Journal*, Vol. 6, No. 2, pp. 109–124. doi:10.2304/eerj.2007.6.2.109.

Howes, D. (1998). "A Spectator's Legacy", *English in Australia*, Vol. 122, pp. 26–30.

Howie, M. (2005). "A Transformative Model for Programming 7–10 English", *English in Australia*, Vol. 142, pp. 57–63.

Howie, M. (2006). "(Un)common Sense: The Case for Critical Literacy", in B. Doecke, M. Howie & W. Sawyer (Eds), *'Only Connect': English Teaching, Schooling and Community*, Adelaide: Wakefield Press, pp. 224–235.

Howie, M. (2023). "Problematizing the 'Problem' of Writing in the NSW Curriculum: A Call for a (Re)turn to Practice", *Curriculum Perspectives*. https://doi.org/10.1007/s41297-023-00221-y.

Kemmis, S. (Ed.) (1981). *The Action Research Reader*, 2nd Edition, Geelong, Victoria: Deakin University.

Kemmis, S. & Mahon, K. (2017). "Coming to 'Practice Architectures': A Genealogy of the Theory", in K. Mahon *et al.* (Eds), *Exploring Education and Professional Practice: Through the Lens of Practice Architectures*, Singapore: Springer, pp. 219–238.

Kidder, T. (1989). *Amongst Schoolchildren*, Boston, MA: Houghton Mifflin.

Kitzhaber, A. et al. (1966). "*What Is English?*" *Working Papers of the Anglo-American Seminar on the Teaching and Learning of English*. Dartmouth College, Hanover, New Hampshire, August 20 – September 16. https://files.eric.ed.gov/fulltext/ED082201.pdf.

Kostogriz, A. & Doecke, B. (2008). "English and its Others: Towards an Ethics of Transculturation", *Changing English*, Vol. 15, No. 3, pp. 259-274. doi:10.1080/13586840802364194.

Lucy, N. (2010). *POMO OZ: Fear and Loathing Downunder*, Fremantle, WA: Fremantle Press.

Luke, A. (2000). "Critical Literacy in Australia: A Matter of Context and Standpoint", *Journal of Adolescent and Adult Literacy*, Vol. 43, No. 5, pp. 448–461.

Macedo, D. (1985). "Rethinking Critical Pedagogy: A Dialogue with Paulo Freire", in P. Freire, *The Politics of Education: Culture, Power and Liberation*, Massachusetts: Bergin & Garvey, pp. 175–199.

MacFarlane, P. (1993). "Garth Boomer, 1940–1993", *Opinion: Journal of the South Australian English Teachers' Association*, Vol. 22, No. 2, pp. 5–7.

Macken-Horarik, M. (2011). "Building a Knowledge Structure for English: Reflections on the Challenges of Coherence, Cumulative Learning, Portability and Face Validity", *Australian Journal of Education*, Vol. 55, No. 3, 197–213.

Mallick, D., Moss, P. & Hansen, I. (Eds) (1982). *New Essays in the Teaching of Literature*, Adelaide: Australian Association for the Teaching of English (AATE).

Manuel, J. (2023). "*'Beacons, Anchors and Liberators for Hard Times': Lasting Lessons from Boomer's Teaching Wisdom*", Garth Boomer Memorial Address, AATE/ALEA National Conference, Canberra, July.

Marine, J., Rogers, P., Blau, S. & Kelly, K. (Eds) (2023). *Toward a Re-Emergence of James Moffett's Mindful, Spiritual, and Student-Centered Pedagogy*, New York: Peter Lang.

Martin, N. (1988). "Introduction", in N. Martin & M. Lightfoot (Eds), *The Word for Teaching Is Learning: Essays for James Britton*, London: Heinemann / Upper Montclair, NJ: Boynton/Cook Publishers, pp. ix–xvii.

Martin, N., Darcy, P., Newton, B. & Parker, R. (1976). *Writing and Learning Across the Curriculum 11–16*, London: Ward Lock Educational.

Mayes, E. (2013). "Negotiating the Hidden Curriculum: Power and Affect in Negotiated Classrooms", *English in Australia*, Vol. 48, No. 3, pp. 62–71.

Mayher, J. (1990). *Uncommon Sense: Theoretical Practice in Language Education*, Portsmouth, NH: Heinemann & Boynton/Cook.

Mayher, J. (2013). "Garth Boomer through an American's Eyes", *English in Australia*, Vol. 48, No. 3, pp. 21–23.

Mayher, J. & Lester, N. (1993). "Goodbye Garth", *English Education*, Vol. 25, No. 3, pp. 188–189.

McClenaghan, D. (1998). "Goodbye Mrs Bell", *English in Australia*, Vol. 122, pp. 6–7.

McKnight, L. (2021). "Since Feeling Is First: The Art of Teaching to Write Paragraphs", *English in Education*, Vol. 55, No. 1, pp. 37–52. doi:10.1080/04250494.2020.1768069.

McLean Davies, L., Doecke, B., Mead, P., Sawyer, W. & Yates, L. (2023). *Literary Knowing and the Making of English Teachers: The Role of Literature in Shaping English Teachers' Professional Knowledge and Identities*, London & New York: Routledge.

McLeod, J. (2014). "Experimenting with Education: Spaces of Freedom and Alternative Schooling in the 1970s", *History of Education Review*, Vol. 43, No. 2, pp. 172–189. doi:10.1108/HER-03-2014-0019.

McLeod, J. & Paisley, F. (2023). "Ambivalent Histories: Education, 'Race', and the Modernisation of Settler/Colonial Governance in Australasia and the Pacific, 1900s–

1960s", *History of Education*, Vol. 52, No. 5, pp. 687–696. doi:10.1080/0046760X.2023.2251928.

Medway, P. (1984). "Doing English Teaching", in M. Meek & J. Miller (Eds), *Changing English: Essays for Harold Rosen*, London: Heinemann Educational, pp. 134–142.

Medway, P. (1990a). "Into the Sixties: English and English Society at a Time of Change", in I.F. Goodson (Ed.), *Bringing English to Order: The History and Politics of a School Subject*, London & Philadelphia: The Falmer Press, pp. 1–46.

Medway, P. (1990b). "Language with Consequences: Worldly Engagement for Critical Inquiry", *English Education*, Vol. 22, No. 3, pp. 147–164.

Medway, P., Hardcastle, J., Brewis, G. & Crook, D. (2014). *English Teachers in a Postwar Democracy: Emerging Choice in London Schools, 1945–1965*, New York & London: Palgrave Macmillan.

Meek, M. (1982). "Response – Begin Again", in D. Mallick, P. Moss & I. Hansen (Eds), *New Essays in the Teaching of Literature*, Adelaide: Australian Association for the Teaching of English (AATE), pp. 85–96.

Misson, R. & Morgan, W. (2006). *Critical Literacy and the Aesthetic: Transforming the English Classroom*, Urbana, IL: National Council of Teachers of English (NCTE).

Mockler, N. (2022). "No Wonder No One Wants to Be a Teacher: World-First Study Looks at 65,000 News Articles About Australian Teachers", *The Conversation*, 11 July. https://theconversation.com/no-wonder-no-one-wants-to-be-a-teacher-world-first-study-looks-at-65-000-news-articles-about-australian-teachers-186210.

Moffett, J. (1981). *Coming on Center: English Education in Evolution*, Montclair, NJ: Boynton/Cook Publishers.

Moffett, J. (1994). *The Universal Schoolhouse: Spiritual Awakening through Education*, San Francisco, CA: Jossey-Bass Publishers.

Moll, L. (2014). *L.S. Vygotsky and Education*, Hoboken, NJ: Taylor and Francis.

Morgan, W. (1992). *A Post-Structuralist English Classroom: The Example of Ned Kelly*, Melbourne: Victorian Association for the Teaching of English (VATE).

Morgan, W. (1997). *Critical Literacy in the Classroom: The Art of the Possible*, London & New York: Routledge.

Moss, P. (1982). "Literacy Culture, Media Culture, Student Culture", in D. Mallick, P. Moss & I. Hansen (Eds), *New Essays in the Teaching of Literature*, Adelaide: Australian Association for the Teaching of English (AATE), pp. 97–111.

NSW Education Standards Authority. (2020). *Teaching Writing – Report of the Thematic Review of Writing*, Sydney: NESA.

Nichols, S. & Cormack, P. (2017). *Impactful Practitioner Inquiry: The Ripple Effect on Classrooms, Schools, and Teacher Professionalism*, New York & London: Teachers College Press.

Noden, P. (1998). "Celebrating Mrs UET!" *English in Australia*, Vol. 122, pp. 5–6.

Onore, C. & Lubetsky, B. (1992). "Why We Learn Is What and How We Learn: Curriculum as Possibility", in G. Boomer, N. Lester, C. Onore & J. Cook (Eds), *Negotiating the Curriculum: Educating for the 21st Century*, London & Washington, DC: The Falmer Press, pp. 243–265.

Pinar, W.F. (2005). "Foreword", in W.F. Pinar & R.L. Irwin (Eds), *Curriculum in a New Key: The Collected Works of Ted. T. Aoki*, Mahwah, NJ: Lawrence Erlbaum Associates, pp. xv–xvii.

Pirie, B. (1997). *Reshaping High School English*, Urbana, IL: National Council of Teachers of English (NCTE).

Priestley, M., Edwards, R. & Priestley, A. (2011). "Teacher Agency in Curriculum Making: Agents of Change and Spaces for Manoeuvre", *Curriculum Inquiry*, Vol. 42, No. 2, pp. 191–214. doi:10.1111/j.1467-873X.2012.00588.x.

Reid, A. (2011). "The Influence of Curriculum Pasts on Curriculum Futures: A South Australian Case Study", in L. Yates, C. Collins & K. O'Connor (Eds), *Australia's Curriculum Dilemmas: State Cultures and the Big Issues*, Melbourne: Melbourne University Press, pp. 45–65.

Reid, A. (2017). "Boomer, Robert Garth (1940–1993)", in *Australian Dictionary of Biography*, Canberra: National Centre of Biography, Australian National University. https://adb.anu.edu.au/biography/boomerrobert-garth-18151/text29726.

Reid, A. (2019). *Changing Australian Education: How Policy Is Taking Us Backwards and What Can Be Done About It*, Sydney: Allen & Unwin.

Reid, I. (1982). "Beyond English and the Classroom", in D. Mallick, P. Moss & I. Hansen (Eds), *New Essays in the Teaching of Literature*, Adelaide: Australian Association for the Teaching of English (AATE), pp. 144–148.

Reid, I. (1984). *The Making of Literature*, Adelaide: Australian Association for the Teaching of English (AATE).

Reid, I. (Ed.) (1987). *The Place of Genre in Learning: Current Debates*, Geelong, Victoria: Centre for Studies in Literary Education, Deakin University.

Reid, J.-A. (2013). "Why Programming Matters: Aporia and Teacher Learning in Classroom Practice", *English in Australia*, Vol. 48, No. 3, pp. 40–45.

Riddle, S. & Apple, W. (2019). *Re-Imagining Education for Democracy*, London & New York: Routledge.

Rose, M. (1989). *Possible Lives: The Promise of Public Education in America*, Boston, MA: Houghton Mifflin.

Sawyer, W. (2008). "English Teaching in New South Wales since 1971: Versions of Growth?" *Changing English*, Vol. 15, No. 3, pp. 323–337. doi:10.1080/13586840802364244.

Sawyer, W. (2013). "A Timely Voice: Garth Boomer on Literature", *English in Australia*, Vol. 48, No. 3, pp. 27–39.

Scholes, R. (1985). *Textual Power: Literary Theory and the Teaching of English*, New Haven, CT & London: Yale University Press.

Schön, D. (1983). *The Reflective Practitioner*, New York: Basic Books.

Snyder, I. (2008). *The Literacy Wars*, Sydney: Allen & Unwin.

Stenhouse, L. (1975). *An Introduction to Curriculum Research and Development*, London: Heinemann Educational Books.

Stroud, G. (2018). *Teacher: One Woman's Struggle to Keep the Heart in Teaching*, Sydney: Allan & Unwin.

Stroud, G. (2023). *The Things That Matter Most*, Sydney: Allen & Unwin.

Taylor, S., Zipin, L. & Brennan, M. (2020). "PTM Curriculum: Putting Knowledge to Work for Communities", *Connect: Supporting Student Participation*, Vol. 242, April, pp. 6–8.

Tchudi, S. (Ed.) (1985). *Language, Schooling and Society*, Upper Montclair, NJ: Boynton/Cook Publishers.

Teese, R. (2014). *For the Common Weal: The Public High School in Victoria 1919–2010*, Melbourne: Australian Scholarly Publishing.

Thomson, J. (1987). *Understanding Teenagers' Reading: Reading Processes and the Teaching of Literature*, North Ryde: Methuen.

Tirrell, M.K. (1990). "James Britton: An Impressionistic Sketch", *College Composition and Communication*, Vol. 41, No. 2, pp. 166–171.

Tremmel, R. (2006). "Changing the Way We Think in English Education: A Conversation in the Universal Barbershop", *English Education*, Vol. 39, No. 1, pp. 10–45.

Tremmel, R. (2010). "On the Horns of a Dilemma: Deweyan Progressivism and English Teacher Education", *English Education*, Vol. 42, No. 2, pp. 121–147.

Tyack, D. & Cuban, L. (1995). *Tinkering Towards Utopia: A Century of Public School Reform*, Cambridge, MA & London: Harvard University Press.

Tyack, D. & Tobin, W. (1994). "The 'Grammar' of Schooling: Why Has it Been so Hard to Change?", *American Educational Research Journal*, Vol. 31, No. 3, pp. 453–479.

Ulmer, G.L. (1985). *Applied Grammatology*, Baltimore, MD & London: The Johns Hopkins University Press.

Vee, A. (2020). "What was the Dartmouth Seminar?" Introduction, Dartmouth '66 Seminar Exhibit. WAC Clearinghouse. https://doi.org/10.37514/TWR-J.2021.1.1.01 https://wac.colostate.edu/repository/exhibits/dartmouth/critical-reflections/what-is-english/.

Weaver, C. (1985). "Parallels Between New Paradigms in Science and in Reading and Literary Theories: An Essay Review", *Research in the Teaching of English*, Vol. 19, No. 3, pp. 298–316.

Wells, G. (1995). "Language and the Inquiry-Oriented Curriculum", *Curriculum Inquiry*, Vol. 25, No. 3, pp. 233–269.

Wells, G. (1999). *Dialogic Inquiry: Towards a Sociocultural Practice and Theory of Education*, Cambridge & New York: Cambridge University Press.

Wildash, H. (2014). "*Garth Boomer: An Educator of His Time – and for All Time*", Garth Boomer Address, AATE/ALEA National Conference, Darwin, July.

Woods, C. (1985). "Zen and the Art of Computing – A Response", in G. Boomer (Ed.), *Fair Dinkum Teaching and Learning: Reflections on Literacy and Power*, Montclair, NJ: Boynton/Cook, pp. 185–187.

Woods, C. (1993). "Garth Boomer – A Celebration", *English in Australia*, Vol. 105, pp. 7–8.

Wyatt-Smith, C. & Jackson, C. (2016). "NAPLAN Data on Writing: A Picture of Accelerating Negative Change", *Australian Journal of Language and Literacy*, Vol. 39, No. 3, pp. 233–244.

Yates, L., Collins, C. & O'Connor, K. (Eds) (2011). *Australia's Curriculum Dilemmas: State Cultures and the Big Issues*, Melbourne: Melbourne University Press.

Young, M.F.D. (Ed.) (1971). *Knowledge and Control: New Directions for the Sociology of Education*, London: Collier Macmillan.

Zipin, L. (2020). "Building Curriculum Knowledge Work Around Community-Based 'Problems That Matter': Let's Dare to Imagine", *Curriculum Perspectives*, Vol. 40, pp. 111–115. https://doi.org/10.1007/s41297-019-00096-y.

Zipin, L. & Brennan, M. (2024). "Opening School Walls to Funds of Knowledge: Students Researching Problems that Matter in Australian Communities", in M. Esteban-Guitart (Ed.), *Funds of Knowledge and Identity Pedagogies for Social Justice: International Perspectives and Praxis from Communities, Classrooms, and Curriculum*, London & New York: Routledge, pp. 41–56.

Index

AATE 1, 16, 64
ACSA 35
action research / teacher as researcher 53–57, 59n18, 59n19
agency (teacher) 7, 38–39;
  and programming 22, 36n16, 59n18;
  student agency vi, 26
assessment 20, 28, 77n18
Australian Schools Commission ix

Barnes, Douglas 73
Barthes, Roland 81
Bernstein, Basil 19, 59n15
Brecht, Bertolt 49–52, 82
Brennan, Marie 27, 28
Britton, James 3–4, 6–10, 14n8, 24, 37, 40, 58n1, 63, 73, 76n1, 77n16
bureaucracy 4, 12, 78–79, 84, 92n10

Comber, Barbara 56–57
'complicity of tact' 49
'composing' 66, 70–72
constraints 21–22, 33, 39
critical literacy 74
cultural literacy 68, 74–75
cultural studies 64–65, 68
curriculum 16–17, 19, 29, 31, 48, 49, 76, 86, 89–91;
  English curriculum x, 3,11, 30ff, 41–62, 68, 69, 75, 87;
  curriculum inquiry ix, xiin1, 16, 30, 36n20;
  curriculum biography ix;
  curriculum composing 16, 23–24, 55;
  curriculum leadership ix, x,12, 78–79;
  curriculum as negotiation 15, 16ff, 25, 29;
  curriculum design (see programming) 22, 23, 25, 59n18;
  curriculum as story 24, 35n15

Curriculum Development Centre ix

Dartmouth viii, 3, 41
Davis, Christine 77n17
Derrida, Jacques 5, 29
Didaktik 14n9, 29, 36n18
Dixon, John 5, 62

'Epic' teacher 51
'estrangement effect' 49–50

genre 72–73, 77n13,
Giroux, Henry 39,
grammar 77n17, 82

Halliday, Michael 63, 71
Hardcastle, John 6

ideology 21 67,
IFTE 1, 11, 15, 43, 53, 65, 66, 69

language across the curriculum x, 8, 30, 53
'language and learning' 5–8, 42, 62, 70;
  and English teaching 31;
  and the 'London School' 4–5
larrikin 88
literature 64, 65, 66, 67
Lucy, Niall 88

Martin, Nancy 35n6, 73
Mayher, John xi, 36n19, 58n6
media 74–75, 95; media and culture 75
Medway, Peter 7
Meek, Margaret 66, 67, 76n4
metaphor 2, 10, 18, 46–47, 95
Moffett, James 90, 92n15

NATE 53
NCTE 43, 46, 58n6, 88, 92n13

'negotiating the curriculum' / curriculum negotiation / negotiation 8, 13, 14n12, 16ff; 30, 31, 36n19;
  as teacher inquiry 55;
  as curriculum composing 16, 25, 28–29, 32, 55;
  negotiation questions 23, 25;
  and student voice 26, 27, 28;
  and democracy 26, 27, 28, 29;
  and Australian Curriculum 28;
  negotiating the English curriculum 30ff;
  'non-negotiables' 35

pedagogy 8–13, 14n9, 23–27, 49–52, 58, 86;
  pedagogic authority 8, 32;
  'pedagogy of the question' 23;
  writing pedagogy 33, 59n18; and the literacy debate 69–74, 82; and policy 83–84;
  English teaching pedagogy 38, 40–41, 63;
  Epic Pedagogy 49–51, 52; 'Epic teacher' 51;
  link between pedagogy and rhetoric 2;
  pedagogy as performance 87–88;
  post-epic pedagogy 47, 52
Post-Dartmouth English teaching 4–6, 40–41, 61–63, 86
postmodern 38, 48, 51
power vi, 19–22, 29, 35n8, 35n9, 35n10

'pragmatic-radical' 39, 40, 48; and 'Epic' teacher 51
'problems that matter' 28
Process:
  in writing 72, 90n1;
  of learning in curriculum 89
process/genre debate 70, 77n14, 82, 83, 90–1n1
'programming' 22–24, 36n16, 56, 59n18;
  programming for learning 25
progressivism 7, 8, 11, 47–48

Reid, Alan 80
Reid, Ian 65
representation 40–45, 50
rhetoric 1–2, 18, 40, 45, 47–48, 84

scholar-practitioner 3–4
Schön, Donald 42
Stenhouse, Lawrence 53, 58n4
subjectivity 6, 38

'teacher power' 13, 39, 53, 58n2
the figure of the teacher 33–34

Vygotsky, Lev 10

Wells, Gordon 36n19
William, Raymond 5, 14n4, 64

Zipin, Lew 28

For Product Safety Concerns and Information please contact our EU representative GPSR@taylorandfrancis.com
Taylor & Francis Verlag GmbH, Kaufingerstraße 24, 80331 München, Germany

www.ingramcontent.com/pod-product-compliance
Lightning Source LLC
Chambersburg PA
CBHW061720300426
44115CB00014B/2759